T0156955

No Room
For A Son

Shirley's Revenge

Marian Wuertz Quaglino

iUniverse, Inc.
Bloomington

No Room For A Son
Shirley's Revenge

iUniverse books may be ordered through booksellers or by contacting:

iUniverse
1663 Liberty Drive
Bloomington, IN 47403
www.iuniverse.com
1-800-Authors (1-800-288-4677)

ISBN: 978-1-4759-0163-4 (sc)
ISBN: 978-1-4759-0164-1 (e)

Printed in the United States of America

iUniverse rev. date: 3/8/2012

DEDICATION

I dedicate this novel to my grand children.
Quinn, Anthony, Lani and Philip, Jr.

PREFACE

My entire morning was out of whack. All that I did seemed to backfire. My stomach was upset, my head hurt, and I felt feverish. Not able to finish the day, I decided to go home, but before getting to the door, Mack called to check on the tiles he needed for a kitchen.

"Mack, I'm glad you called," I said. "your tiles are in the store room, my stomach is giving me hell, frankly, Mack, I'd like to go home. Will you open the office tomorrow and consider overtime? I may need more than a day to get myself together."

Mack was sympathetic. "Go home, Ryan take care of yourself. I'll handle tomorrow. If you need more time, let me know."

Mack was not just a reliable foreman, he was my fathers best friend, and with a large swig of Maalox in mind, I locked the office.

On the way home, my mind wandered. Blaming my horrendous past, the thought has been in my head for years. Is Edward really my son? Attentively, the child has called me "dad," which he thinks is so, none the less, belonging is part of the battle, Raising Edward for eight years, my outlook is better, we are family now. Andrea is a wonderful wife and mother, Millie is an endless treasure, and digging into *how it all started, I know the truth.* The child that I denied is *truly my son.*

No Room For A Son

CHAPTER ONE

"What's wrong, my love?" my wife asked." Is there a problem? You're home early."

"I'm all right, my dear," I said, "just a little stomach disorder, wrestling with a hot roof took the starch out of me. I'd like to sleep for a while and have something light for supper."

The cold shower that I had in mind went astray, pipes were unusually warm, but soaping generously, I got rid of grime. Lacking that refreshed feeling, I slipped into short pajamas, crawled into bed, and lying to my left, the beat of my heart was more than rapid. Tylenol helped, but I could not relax. Pacing the floor, a picture on the bureau caught my eye, centered in a class of 165 graduates, my brother bloomed like a rose.

June 15, 1955, Ralph pranced into the den wearing, what seemed to be a nightshirt. Draped in the unusual garb, mom praised his appearance and lending way to the style show, dad left the comfort of his favorite chair.

"Congratulations, son," he said clasping Ralph's hand, "you look grand! This is a day you will remember for the rest of your life, mother and I are proud."

Overcome with sentiment, dad flipped the tear that he had so desperately been trying to hide, mom had probably enacted her conformities earlier, and putting my two cents in, naturally, I goofed.

"What's with the black nightgown, Ralph?" I asked flippantly.

Ralph did not answer, and accepting the distasteful look for what it was worth, I kept my mouth shut. Loyola University was our goal, this much, I knew, but the silly-looking hat that Ralph wore had me baffled. The family was excited, Ralph seemed elated, and to avoid the flurry, I went to my room.

"Have Gun Will Travel," was my favorite program. The name "Paladin" seemed to fit, Richard Boone may have thought so too, and why not admit, the moniker did have charisma. Watching from my bed, Paladin rallied triumphantly, and glancing over my shoulder, dad was watching me from the door.

"Ryan," he said, pointing a finger. "Tonight is your brother's big night, commencement begins at 7:00, and you are wasting time. If you don't get a move on we may not get seats near the rostrum. Now, get to the bathroom!"

Commencement was bad enough, but that other word threw me.

"Dad, what's a "rostrum?" I asked.

"That's another word meaning "stage" son," he barked. "You're slowing things down, Ryan. Get moving."

Mom came with my blue pants draped over her arm, she had just pressed the crease, and scrounging in my closet, she chose a white shirt and blue tie.

"Here are your clothes, Ryan," she said. "Wear blue sox with your blue sport jacket and don't forget to pass a brush on your shoes. You should dress now, your father wants to leave no later than 6:00 o'clock."

Hurrying my bath, I dressed as fast as I could, running a brush through my hair the troublesome cowlick in the middle of my head wouldn't stay put, and ignoring the defiant sprig, I ran downstairs. Ralph looked pissed, he blamed me of course, and rushing me into the car, I bumped my head.

The auditorium was beginning to crowd, my hickey was starting to throb, Ralph hurried inside, and looking ahead, Dad directed us to the first row just beyond a section marked "reserved."

The "rostrum" was in full view. Getting an early start, dad made sure of that, but whatever the occasion, the stage seemed a bit unusual. Six American flags were the center of attention, a row of chairs and a table piled with rolls of parchment did nothing to inflate one's imagination, and wondering what the evening might bring, impatiently, I wiggled in a seat that didn't just wobble, it squeaked. Short of biting my nails, I was never so bored, the passing hour seemed more like three when, suddenly, the band excelled to a march that nearly popped my ears. One hundred and sixty-five graduates paraded in the aisles wearing headpieces that that I have never seen. The extreme doodad was shaped like a bowl, with the bottom glued to to a cardboard square and cagily, attached, a yellow tassel jiggled at the turn of every head.

"Gee, mom, "why is everybody wearing those funny looking hats?" I asked.

Mom gave me a wicked look, and knowing what that meant, I sat, tolerating throbs from a pointless hickey.

A graduate that mom said was the "Valtidor," or whatever, talked a long time. Professors had a lot to say, and with rambling bigwigs using the balance of time, graduates were finally extolled. A sheepskin of merit was unquestionably the backbone of commencement, and naturally, the best is last. Of course, I was fidgety, any ten-year old would be, three hours of theatrical prattle was more than I had expected, and when the ruckus was over, my hickey made me do it.

"What kind of hat is that, Ralph?" I asked critically.

Angrily shaking his forefinger, my brother lashed,

"Ryan," he said, annoyed, "this is not a hat. It's a mortarboard! This outfit dates back to the 17th century and before. It's tradition, imp! Don't knock it! If ever you graduate, the proverbial brick might fall on your head!"

Ten years old, and full of beans, it seemed, I goaded Ralph a second time, chastising rather prickly, I did not appreciate the pointed finger in my face, but understanding the value of a civil tongue, I was embarrassed silly.

June 18, 1960, was my special night. Reflecting before the full length mirror in mom's bedroom, the four-cornered square fit fine, dangling at the side of my face, the traditional yellow tassel reigned supreme, and tingling to the significance of graduation, credit goes to Ralph. My brother was right! Twelve years of education is a prelude to common sense and chivalry. What I have learned, I intend improving. Knowledge and wisdom opens the door to maturity, responsibility, and competence. In cemetery silence, I studied until my eyes burned, my brain retains knowledge, but the imposing garb means more than what I have achieved. June 18, 1960, will remain a proud day in my life, and there's more. Graduating at the head of my class, I was endorsed with honor, my parents were proud, and gaining my brother's respect, I was on cloud nine.

"Valedictorian," is not easy to come by, and dwelling on the past, my prom had kinks that I will never forget.

CHAPTER TWO

Seven o'clock, on a Saturday, prom night, finally, grappled through the calendar. I called for Carol at 6:30 and seeing her so fashionably decked, the surprise bit of panache blew my mind, never before had I realized Carol was so lovely. Always, we were together, and not wanting a "steady," I considered her a buddy in blue jeans. Carol was rugged, she liked to fish, running a hook through a grasshopper didn't bother her, she scaled the day's catch in nothing flat and played a mean game of chess. Adorned with the frills of a Monarch, my romping caterpillar was never so lovely, and falling apart with the unexpected, I was tuned to the likes of man.

Reaching the entrance of my Alma Mater, Pete Lester's five piece crew played my kind of music. Rushing Carol to the dance floor, I held her close, but switching to high jive, the band threw me. Knowing I was uncomfortable, Carol grinned and taking my hand we headed to the punch bowl.

"Well, Ryan, this formal is a far cry from blue jeans," she said, "Are you pleased?"

"Carol, you look great! Off shoulder fashion complements you," and gazing at her bosom, I added, "that hint of cleavage would turn anybody on."

"Ha! That's a first," she said, and grinning triumphantly, she knew the gown was right.

Gathered at the punch bowl, Jim Leonard asked rather stunned.

"Ryan Daniels, where have you been hiding this lovely girl? You look great Carol! Come with me, my pretty, this number is for us," and before knowing, my date was swinging to the Jitterbug.

Left alone, I strolled towards the entrance looking for Ben. He arrived five minutes later and seeing his arm wrapped around Shirley Freeman I, was more than surprised.

"Hi Ryan," he said. "I'm sure you know Shirley."

"Not personally. Hi, Shirley," I said.

Searching the dance floor, Ben seemed puzzled and squinting his brow, he asked. "Is that Carol dancing with Jim?"

"Sure is, Ben, she floored me too," and winking assuredly, I added. "I'm looking from a different angle now."

I grew up with Benjamin Rollins. Two years my senior, we jelled, and somewhere along the way, I had shortened his name to "Ben." Ralph was well on his way in medical school, married two years, I hardly saw him, and pairing like peas in a pod, Ben and I were inseparable.

"What kept you, Ben?" I asked, "you've lost nearly forty-five minutes," and little knowing what was to come, Ben poked fun at this date.

"You know the fancy primping that girls do," he teased.

I'm sure Ben didn't mean that as a smear, The remark was merely toned with toned with humor, but Shirley spat sarcasm.

"Well," she growled, "you didn't have to bring me. I have no problem getting dates."

"Shirley, please, don't take things to heart," Ben apologized. "I was kidding. You fly off the handle too fast."

"Maybe I do," she remarked. "I have no use for that kind of kidding."

Her behavior was callous. Ben didn't need sarcasm, and to top all, she ignored me. Meeting Shirley for the first time, I considered she was pretty. Flirting around campus, I understood why fellows looked her way, but raking Ben over the coals, I have no use for flippancy.

The "Jolly Boys" were at their loudest, Shirley, hauled Ben to the dance floor, and putting two with two, I had no earthly reason to like the girl. Stan and Carol were doing nicely with the jitterbug, usually, the had an audience, but the Jitterbug was not my style. Loosing track of Carol, I caught Shirley flirting over Ben's shoulder, Norman Porter was her target, and ceding to the lusty come-on, he wasted no time cutting in. Ben was not pleased, irately, he crossed the floor keeping a watchful eye. Jim Wilson staged a cut-in, but involved with Norman Porter, Shirley slighted the guy.

Ben was not happy, and noticing the disappointment, I put my foot in my mouth

"Ben," I confronted, "why would you want to date the most talked about girl on campus? Shirley is attractive, but the girl travels in a fast lane. Haven't you heard the gossip?

"Ryan, that's just what it is, gossip," Ben said sharply. "Shirley hasn't been around long enough to develop a reputation."

"Ahh! Come off it, fellow," I said. "Shirley spreads lies all over, she's loose and flirty. I've heard that from at least a dozen guys."

Ben glared wildly, and aware of timely anger, the thought dawned, my buddy had a crush on Shirley.

"OK, Ryan," he said sharply. "How do you rate with Shirley?"

What I said was not at all delicate. Provoking my best friend, I deserved what he dished. I didn't know Shirley, intimately, that is, and governed by hearsay, I was wrong.

"I asked a question!" Ben lashed. "Tell me, Ryan! How do you rate with Shirley?"

"Ah, come off it Ben. You well know that doesn't include me. What you've just said isn't fair. If Shirley is what you want, go for it."

Touching marrow, I incited Ben, and with the rift getting prickly, I was not comfortable.

According to rumor, the Freeman family came to New Orleans just weeks before campus enrollment. Working for an oil company in Lafayette, Shirley's father was transferred, and taking gossip for granted, the way I see it now, the wolf pack could have damaged Shirley's reputation.

Stan, finally returned with my date, and with rhythm fitting my style, I danced with Carol. But knowing their way around music, the "Jolly Boys" spiced the tune to Jitterbug jive. Damning all, I adlibbed, and accommodating a cut-in, I was not disappointed.

Crossing the floor, someone tapped my shoulder.

"Hi, Fred," I said turning. "Who's the pretty girl with you?"

"Knowing Fred Kelly's little sister, I teased. The young miss blushed and Fred rambled an explanation.

"Adelaide has just turned sixteen, and don't criticize when I tell you her nick-name is "Lady."

"Why, Fred, the nickname fits. You should bring "Lady" to the Saturday night hops. But why aren't you with Shelia?"

"Sheila is in New York with her parents, they're visiting relatives," he said. "I've been teaching my sister to dance, Mom worked all of last week sewing her first formal, and tonight, I'm her guy."

Fred flashed a wink soliciting my service. I put the punch bowl on hold and searching the floor, I figured Fred was looking for Carol. My girl was cool with fast numbers, and the Jitterbug kept her occupied.

"Ryan," Fred said, "I don't know the dude dancing with Carol, but his version of the Jitterbug is a little on the tango side. Wouldn't you say your date is a bit uncomfortable?"

"Maybe so, Fred. When I left the floor she was dancing with Jim Barnes. You and Carol pair pretty good with the Jitterbug. Go ahead, Carol likes that kind of rhythm."

"I'm going to cut in, Ryan, and heed the warning, pal, I'm going to keep her a while." Fred was one of the best, he liked hot rhythm, nothing compared with his style and Carol was his favorite partner.

Fred's little sister was quite pretty. Mature trappings over ranked her age, and I didn't mind. Tapping her feet to rhythm, she seemed anxious to crash the floor, I waited for r a number that I could be comfortable with, and Glenn Miler's "String of Pearls," was the topper. Sensing the tempo my young partner swayed to the tune with panache. James Lawton seemed to pursue "Lady" all during the evening, and noticing the many cut-ins, something was beginning to brew.

Fred, having Carol under his wing, I would be alone for a while, I wasn't too happy about that, but glancing at fellows around the punch bowl, Brad Johnson pointed to his cup. Brad was a well known prankster, many of his escapades backfired, and today, I'd be willing to bet he spiked the punch.

Ben did not mingle, but as prom nights prolong, variety crossed paths at midnight, Shirley, it seemed, had talked Ben into a romp in the French Quarter.

"Why don't you two come with us?" Ben asked. "Pat O'Brien's bar should be fun. I'd like to try one of those famous "Hurricanes."

The offer seemed genuine enough, but Carol was hungry, I could eat too, and rejecting the deal we drove to the Rockery Inn.

CHAPTER THREE

Two thirds of the graduating class was there, the place buzzed like a hornets nest, and after a fifteen minute wait, the hostess led us to a table.

Carol ordered fried chicken with fries, I had the same with baked potato and between bites, we discussed the prom. A stickler for music, Carol praised Bob Lennon's solo, and mulling through the mayhem that had happened, I was disappointed.

Leaving the Rockery at 3:00 in the morning, I parked in Carol's drive between two rows of shrubbery. The neighborhood was quite, and looking for the usual goodnight kiss on the cheek, Carol seemed sugary.

"Thank you, Ryan, the evening was wonderful, I've had a lovely time, and Ryan," she paused smiling, "I like being with you."

Her eyes were inviting, sulky to say the least and sensing desire, she kissed my mouth sliding her tongue between my lips.

"You're sweet, Carol" I whispered, "I like having you with me."

Compulsive kissing seemed to turn her on. I was bothered too, and taking the situation for granted, I slipped my hand under her gown, Ripping fragile panties, her breath came in gasps, my blood raced, and swollen with desire, I yanked the zipper in my pants. Carol released her legs, she seemed to want sex, and forcing hard, I could not penetrate the velvety template of an untouched virgin.

"Stop Ryan," she begged. Don't do this!"

"I'm sorry, Carol, I thought you wanted this. I have condoms in the glove compartment," I quickly mentioned.

"I'm sure you do, Ryan, but you hurt me. I've never had sex. You should know that now. I feel the need, but I can't let it happen. The man I marry deserves more."

Her stare penetrated to the back of my head, then, serious as all get out, she lashed. "Tell me, Ryan. Do I really have a chance with you?"

The remark caught me off guard, I had no reasonable answer. "Be patient with me, Carol," I mumbled. "I'm not ready for commitment."

"I'm not asking for marriage, Ryan," she said, testily, "I just want to know where I stand," then, nodding reluctantly, her attitude changed.

"Good night, Ryan!" she muttered, "thank you for a lovely evening."

Apparently, peeved, and perhaps, dampened with uncertainty, Carol got out of the car. Thinking of what had happened at the prom, I felt responsible, first, it was Ben, and now, Carol. I was stung twice, and to embellish a lavish, sexual let-down, a cold shower was better than nothing.

The next time I saw Ben, he seemed aloof. Perhaps, after two weeks, it could be, he hoarded a grudge, and rehashing the episode, I should apologize, but twenty-four hours later, he set things straight.

"Hi, Ryan," he said, standing at my door with the rented tux over his shoulder. "I'm returning my tux today. Why don't we go together, and later, get something to eat? I've been at the store all this week until late, if I don't do this today, I may never have a better time."

"Thanks, Ben," I said, "I've brought mine back, but I'll go with you. My parents are going to a movie this evening, left-over food is not enticing, but let me take my care, my tank is low."

"That'll work," Ben said. "Mr. Carlo and dad are working with a crew of auditors. I left early, and dad will be tied up until late."

Spreading the tux over the back seat, seemingly, all was forgotten, Ben had refreshed friendship, and it was good to renew comfort.

"What's with the camera on the back seat? Do you have pictures to develop?" Ben asked.

"Think about it Ben." I said, starting my car, "I've been carrying that just in case. "Why don't we visit our Alma Mater? Today could very well be the last time."

"You're right, Ryan. That building is alive with memories. I'm glad you have the camera, we can take a few last minute shots."

I filled my tank at a local Shell, crossed Elysian Fields Avenue, then, waiting for a red light, Shirley Freeman stopped her car alongside mine. She had to be following when I left the station, and before I knew, Ben was under siege. Shirley played the field, I saw that at the prom. True, or otherwise, most of the guys had opinions, mine were rigid, and giving thought to a blooming idea, Ben was a victim, snagged in a Venus Flytrap with Shirley controlling the hinge.

"Where are you guys headed?" She asked throwing Ben a cocky wink, but Shirley didn't have to ask, with a tuxedo over the back seat, she knew, and snapping at the bait, Ben explained.

"I'm returning my tux, and we're going to the campus to take pictures."

"Well, that's a coincidence. I'm going there too," she said. "Can we go together? I'll park my car and on the way back we can stop for a coke at Beekman's drug store."

Ben was overjoyed having Shirley around. We snapped an entire roll and though I resented her presence, she was handy snapping pictures of two friends that had graduated together. After that toxic coke, an alluring conspiracy seemed to develop. I hardly saw Ben. Shirley invited him to her home for dinner, Ben dated her constantly, and with prime time encouragement, Ben was head over heels in love.

Two weeks before Christmas, Ben slipped a diamond ring on her finger, and ever since, Shirley's plans were easy.

Looking forward to Christmas Holidays, I half-way hoped we might have a little time together, Ben was never evasive, not with me, I simply believed that Shirley was deliberately keeping him out of circulation, but as time passed, he didn't strain himself being friendly.

Hardly noticing Christmas, the New Year terribly void, and with Mardi Gras just six weeks ahead, I wondered about that. Dad, a member of the Babylon organization for twenty years, never failed inviting Ben and his date to the ball. At Tony's Tableau, on Canal Street, we were always together renting tuxedos, and engaged for just six weeks, the apparent change in Ben had me baffled. Calling the store several times, Ben was never there, and prone to his protective way with Shirley, I thought that somewhere I may have said what I shouldn't. I was concerned, and for the sake of my conscience, I hashed things with Carol.

"Oh, Ryan, don't hallucinate," she lectured. "Ben's wrapped in wedding plans, give him time."

But there was never a call. Dad had reserved a table for six, and to be on the safe side, I put the invitations in Ben's mail-box.

The ball was scheduled for 8:00 p.m. on a Saturday night, Dad had to leave early for rehearsal, and with no word from Ben, I was disappointed.

Pomp and circumstance reigned as usual, I was not interested. Looking for Ben, an hour put a dent in time, and as hope waned, I pictured the collapse of foursome dating. Carol's desire for dancing left me at the table more times than I had bargained for, and when dad was busy with call-outs, I danced with my mom. Ben's behavior was rather callous, and after two hours of neck stretching, I threw in the towel.

Things were not kosher, and not wanting to discuss the the stand off by phone, I watchede stand=off by phone. I met Ben in the drivthings over the phone, I waited in the drive, friendship was not kosher, I had to know why, and watching for him to park in the drive, I confronted him.

"Ben, I asked, "will you have supper with me this evening?" I think we should talk."

"Of course, Ryan. Tonight is a good time," he said off handedly.

The line at the A&G moved slowly, Ben seemed fidgety, and concerned with a riff that had no meaning, I whispered over his shoulder.

"Ben, you've been rather cool lately. Mom asked if you were ill when you didn't show at the ball. I didn't know what to tell her, and believe me, I'm baffled. Have I done something to irritate you."

"Of course you haven't, Ryan," he said, "I'm stuck with wedding plans. Shirley is excited, but for me, it's a bunch of humbug."

"Carol said that might be the reason, but you're moody Ben. you've been avoiding me like a plague. I think we should talk. Ben turned away, sighing in a depth of despair, he looked beaten and worn. Surely, my friend was burdened.

"Look at me Ben," I said, "tell me what's wrong."

Selecting a nearby booth, more than likely, Ben didn't care to eat, pushing food around his plate he appeared dejected.

"We had fun, Ben." I said quickly. "You missed a good time, and we missed you. Things weren't the same," then, reluctantly adding, I said, "Ben, you could have called."

"Ryan, I'm sorry. Have patience with me. I'm running into problems, and there's one that bothers me."

"That's OK, Ben, just talk to me. We've always confided, but with marriage on your mind, I suppose things will be different."

Playfully, nudging his chin with my fist, I hoped that Ben would relax, but anxiety appeared deeply rooted, obviously, he was not in a talkative mood, and feeling rather foolish, I casually asked. "Have you two set a date?"

"Not yet, Ryan. That's up to Shirley," he shrugged. "I seem to be left out."

Ben dallied listlessly playing with his food then, after a deep breath, he flared.

"Shirley wants to wait until June, but that's too far off for me. Her mother was married in June," and coming across defeated, Ben said crossly. "That's traditional crap, and not only that, she wants to be with relatives in Covington on Carnival Day. Her aunt is celebrating 25 years of marriage."

I got the message. Ben would not be around during Mardi Gras.

"You're my best friend, Ryan," he stumbled on, "I wanted you to stand up with me, but Shirley wants her brother. David is fifteen years old, he's just a kid. I've tried to make her see it my way, but she won't budge."

"Forget it, Ben," I said, "you're committed to responsibility now. Let's face it buddy, we're not kids anymore. I'll miss you, Ben, but when things change, we have to respect that,"

Ben was not the guy I once knew. His face was fatigued, wan and fragile, he was void of enthusiasm, had no sense of humor, and disturbed, I wondered, How much is he hiding?

"Thanks for the kind words, Ryan, but this is a different orb for me. Maybe I'm sensitive, I love her Ryan, and I want to be with her." We're fast friends, but doing the town like we used to" Ben hesitated, "I don't think so."

"Just be happy, buddy." I winked assuredly.

With the few bites that Ben put in his mouth, obviously, he did not enjoy supper. The evening proved zilch, nothing was accomplished and leaving the cafeteria, I imagined, Ben could be facing a rocky future. He loved Shirley, that was evident, but Shirley's portals were cluttered. Digging into reason, Ben and Shirley had nothing in common. Ben was considerate, sensuous, and kind, Shirley was nefariously cold, quick tempered and rude, with nothing between, Ben might drift into a spontaneous lapse of gloom?

CHAPTER FOUR

Mardi Gras was on the rocks, Ben's wedding blew that, but should a foursome become fact, actually, I would not be at ease.

The following Saturday, Carol and I were in the Quarter looking for places to spook on Mardi Gras Day. Moseying with crowds, we enjoyed the River walk and browsing for nearly an hour, our stomachs pinched.

Choosing the Court of Two Sisters, Carol ordered lobster; a first for her, I ordered porterhouse steak and knowing that Carol was friendly with Shirley, curiosity had it's way.

"Carol." I asked, "for the life of me, I can't understand why Ben is so attracted to Shirley. Do you think she really loves him?"

"Huh," Carol shrugged vaguely, "do you want opinion, analysis, or fact?" She laughed rather shrewdly.

"Go ahead, Carol, laugh." I said, "I ask because I'm concerned. Ben loves that girl so much he has trouble seeing what she's made of. My opinion doesn't give her much credit, I just want to know how she registers with you?"

"Look Ryan, Ben's a nice guy, he's sensitive, friendly and considerate, Shirley is OK, she's just wicked, but Ben deserves more." Carol frankly remarked.

"I know that, Carol," I said, "just answer my question."

"All right, maybe this is what you're fishing for."

Nodding rather negatively, Carol let loose. "Shirley told me that she and Norman Porter are intimately involved, but Norman has denied that. I'm telling you because you and Ben are good friends, but please, Ryan, don't repeat this."

"Carol, I have no intention telling Ben or anyone, just remember, girls gossip as well as guys."

What Carol said didn't surprise me, I've been around the block with Shirley's inventive quirks, especially noticing hanker when she gawks at my thighs. It's known that Shirley is untruthful. What Carol had just told me, I did not doubt, but Ben loves her enough to take her for his wife, and I will not strengthen what I have always imagined.

Two weeks later, the eccentric day emerged, but not with promise. Sun had warmed the streets by 10:00 o'clock, but Mardi Gras and spicy aspects on Bourbon Street did not excite me. I missed Ben.

Romping the Quarter with Carol, I was not enthused, Bourbon Street, faggots ruled the day. Sensing Carol's discomfort, I avoided the hordes, but ballyhooing with Ben it was different, We coveted the off color clichés soaking up beer and sexual urge. Mardi Gras was our day, we rambled loose and fancy free collaborating with girls that we would never see a second time, and closing the shutters, we satisfied our stomachs with fried chicken and fries. A cold glass of milk was the topper, and just before dawn, we were in bed satisfied and sober.

We had good times, Ben and I, but tying the knot with Shirley, I had doubts. When we first met, I didn't like the girl, and judging her manners at the prom, I refuse to believe that Shirley is right for Ben.

The next six months seemed to fly. Ben hadn't been around too much, and unhappily, the perilous day crawled into my life. June 10, 1962, Ben and Shirley were married.

The weather was lousy. Blizzard like gales scattered misty drizzles and guests scurried through the spurts. The hall was crowded, champagne corks popped by the dozen, waiters struggled between the crowd toting trays, camaraderie buzzed noisily, and away from the crowd, I spotted the impatient groom nervously pacing the foyer.

Displaying charm, the scene was convincing. Ben's bride stood at the top of the stairs ready to toss her bouquet. Carol maneuvered to catch the nosegay, but was disappointed when tall, Ruby Nelson snatched the sailing ritual. For my part, the entire affair dragged, I had a terrific headache, and at the final hour, Ben ditched the tux for a blue suit. Minutes later, Shirley was seen running down the stairs wearing a blue, two-piece suit. Scrambling to the exit, the newlyweds were clobbered with green rice, roughish friends had tied tin cans and trashy shoes to the bumper of Ben's Grand Prix, and the "Just Married" rant was scribbled over the hood. Leonard Faust had Ben in a bear hug. Surrounded by well-wishers, my buddy wallowed in glory. He seemed exuberant, and leaving him to wallow in special glory, I wanted seclusion. Ducking behind a column, I didn't have to smoke, but catering to habit, I hardly had the cigarette in my mouth when Shirley confronted me holding a lighter with an open flame. This, I didn't need and walking away, Shirley was swift. Cupping my face, she pressed a hard kiss to my mouth, I pushed her aside and through clenched teeth, she warned.

"Ryan," her eyes traveled to my groin, "nothing is sacred, just give me time. I'll get to see what's behind that zipper."

Shirley knew what she was, seemed to like what she stood for, and I was never able to figure the focus on me.

By now, well-wishers had thinned. Ben crossed the court yard, taking luggage from the trunk of his car, and closing the lid, he gazed hopelessly at devastating tripe.

"Wait up, Ryan," he called to me.

"Will you follow dad home? We'll be in the lemo behind you. It's not my intention to insult the fellows, but I can't park this eyesore at the airport. Will you drive us there?"

"Of course, Ben." I grinned. "I'll gladly do that."

Twenty minutes later, Mr. Rolling hugged his son ever so mightily. Slipping an envelope is Ben's top pocket, he gave Shirley a nicely wrapped gift and adding my two cents, I embraced the best pal I ever had. Not knowing what Shirley would do, she had it figured. Forcibly, turning my face to hers, Shirley, kissed me, her teeth cut my lip and backing away, she laughed.

"I don't think you've been kissed like that before, Ryan," she said tersely, "just stay cool, your time will come."

Naturally, Ben didn't get it, he merely smiled, and what his father had in mind, I'll never know.

Quiet and rather grim on the way home, Ben's father could have been thinking of the rigid bond they shared, like two kids they were always together, playing football, basket ball, golf, and swimming. Competing in yearly events, without a doubt, they enjoyed togetherness, and knowing the height of companionship, I saw a man being pulled apart.

"I've never, been there, Ryan," he prattled, "I hear Las Vegas is a fun town. Ben seemed high-spirited looking forward to his first flight, but Shirley seemed to take things for granted. I expect she's flown before now."

Small talk, that's what it was, and half listening, my mind turned to yesteryear.

Ten years ago, the Rollins family moved in the house next to mine, the supermarket was soon to open, and within a few days their two-story, nine room brick home was certainly not an eyesore to the neighborhood. Before the wedding, Ben's father had converted the four top rooms to a private apartment. Scanning the neighborhood for potential real estate, Shirley didn't like that, but Ben explained. With no rental fee, they could save extra cash, and having a yen for money, Shirley agreed.

Two weeks seemed to fly. When the newlyweds came home, I leaned to a quick "hello," that did not happen, there was no phone call and friendship seemed to fade. Feeling like a twin without a sibling, my mind wandered to the Black Orchard where we made plans that could never be, and how could I forget the many Saturdays at the super market when I was twelve standing on a box stacking cans on a shelf over my head? I liked working with Ben, and always, before closing, his father shoved a ten-dollar bill in my pocket. I remember 1958 when his mother had died, and how we spent that sorrowful time together. I was there for him, his parents were good to me, and I would never have it any other way. We bloomed like brothers. The first week after Ben had graduated I witnessed gratitude when his father handed built-in security, Ben was promoted to "Manager" sharing part of the store's yearly profits. Mr. Rollins raised his salary, and after a few months, Ben managed the store on his own. I remember driving with him to the bank, Ben had been saving since he was ten, and just before the wedding, he told me that he had $17,000.00 in his savings account. Ours, was a tailored role, binding friendship that I thought, was impossible to sever, and today, we are strangers.

Sadly, thinking of the past, time and circumstance had altered my life, At times. I was distraught, then again, there was actual hurt and to ignore the divide, I crammed idle time with work.

Daniels & Son, Incorporated was heavily committed, working as usual, I did anything to hasten jobs. Tacking sheet-rock, I sized the surface, and finalizing blueprints, I implemented landscape. Ben made no attempt to rejuvenate a soiled alliance, the rift had me disturbed, and pounding nails into a 2X4, I wondered why.

With curiosity getting to me, I called a few times, and not wanting to become involved, when Shirley answered, I hung up. Five months seemed to fly, accepting Ben's standoffish attitude, I considered the incident foul and plunged headfirst into work. But Shirley bothered me too, I cannot forget that offensive kiss and the churlish remark she dished the day of her wedding.

Stuck with skepticism and hurt, I worked overtime dubbing new ideas on blueprints and mitered enough molding to finish six screened doors. Taking time for lunch, I wasn't too hungry, and biting into a healthy chunk of pizza, I was surprised to see my friend walk into the office.

"Hello, Ben," I said, "it's good to see you," and knowing the guy so well, I knew he was disturbed.

"It's been quite a while, buddy, almost six months." I emphasized.

"Ryan. I regret that. I've missed you too, and I do feel foolish." Looking around, he nervously asked. "Are you alone?"

"Yes, Ben," I said. "dad is in the Lake View area with Mike, and the crew won't be back until 5:00 this evening."

My estranged friend looked sick, and baffled, I said, "Ben, you seem troubled. Do you want to talk?"

Ben has always been a lighthearted guy, but something was in the wind. Coming to my office after so long a time,

I didn't know what to expect, then, taking two Regals from the fridge I popped the caps handing a bottle to Ben.

"If something is bothering you buddy, and you think I can help, talk to me," I said abruptly. but looking steadily at the floor, Ben seemed to be thinking. Calmly, I waited, not saying a word, then, glaring into space, angrily he bellowed .

"Ryan, I have a tub of trouble."

Like a child made to stand in a corner, my buddy wallowed in hurt, then, nervously rolling the brown bottle between his palms, his voice softened.

"Ryan, I have to talk. We've always hashed problems with each other, and this, I will not take to my father. Ryan," he hopelessly nodded, "I'm in a mess of trouble."

"Let's go to the back Ben," I said, "we'll be comfortable on the old sofa. I'll disconnect the phone and lock the door."

Ben lit a cigarette, reached for the ashtray at the top of the refrigerator, and pacing the floor he expelled swells of smoke. Whatever was on his mind had to weigh heavily, and hesitating to to explain, I, lost patience.

"Ben," I said aggravated. "Get it out of your gut, Ben, whatever is troubling you, if I can help, I'll damned well try."

I lit a cigarette too, and with Ben staring steadily at the floor, the listless retreat made me edgy.

"Come off it Ben! Cut the crap! What in hell is going on?"

"Ryan," he groaned, "Shirley and I are having trouble. We're married just five months, and already she's gone through the money that I've been saving since I was a kid. I don't know how to handle her Ryan, we argue a lot, and always, it's about money."

"Gosh, Ben, I hardly know what to say. I remember when you told me about the 17,000.00 dollars you had saved. Is all of that gone?"

"Damned near, pal. She bought two mink coats in Vegas, and a diamond watch to boot. The Honeymoon cost a bundle, I've paid the biggest part of the wedding and racked out $2,600.00 for her ring. I shouldn't have done that," and with second thoughts, he mumbled, "I think that's what gave her the idea I was loaded."

Lighting a second cigarette from the first, his voice seemed to crack. "Ryan," he mumbled, "you know dad has always been fair, he raised my salary when we were married, but it's never enough. I just can't handle Shirley's spending."

"I don't know what to tell you, Ben. This is something I shouldn't butt into. Give marriage time, Ben. I'm sure things will get better."

"Don't misunderstand, Ryan. I don't expect anyone to solve my problems, but Shirley gets mean, I can't handle her, just last week she threw a clock at me."

"OK, Ben, here's where I put my foot in my mouth, why don't you limit what she spends?"

"I've done that, Ryan. We've been fighting ever since. Dad gave us 2,000.00 dollars at the airport, he paid for our trip to Vegas, he turned three rooms into a private apartment at his expense. Our place is nice. We don't pay rent or buy groceries, Shirley takes what we need from the store, but it's never enough."

Ben gazed into space, then looking directly at me he said something that was none of my affair.

"Ryan, she turns her back when we're in bed."

That, was something I didn't care to know, and getting to Shirley, I'm sure, the girl was more drawn to Super Market assets rather than the man she married.

"I had to talk to someone, Ryan," Ben said getting to his feet, "my chest was full, spilling my guts, I feel better, and thanks for putting up with me."

Talking as always, Ben may have been relieved, but tightening his grip as we shook hands, he said what could very well be a one-sided wish. "Ryan, if she would just meet me half-way."

Ben was never a coward, but weak-willed as I've seen today, I hardly recognized the friend I grew up with. Valuing his friendship, is easy, but I will not inherit his sticky demean. I will not degrade Shirley, Ben loves her too much, and lacking courage, my innate friend will never defy the allegations of a contentious wife.

Pushing the Rollins problem to the back of my mind, two months seemed to fly from the calendar. The weather was so cold even Jack Frost might consider the warmth of a raccoon coat. Snow, in New Orleans was a rarity, but on February 12, 1964, roofs were heavily laden. Icicles dripped to twelve inches in length, and firmly positioned in white splendor, the kids had a ball making snowmen.

CHAPTER FIVE

Except for an occasional "hello" in the drive, Ben was aloof, and I knew why. Foul, sarcastic bitching traveled in the dead of night. Coping with his insidious wife, Ben let Shirley have her way and not thinking much of his devil may care attitude, I considered him sheepish.

In a way, Ben and I were reared much alike. Just as he had worked with his father, my dad took me under his wing pounding into my skull the essentials of contracting. Just as Ben had saved, I did too, and having a tidy sum, marriage was far from my mind, especially after witnessing the mess that Ben had to cope with.

Surely, I had a crush on Carol, but can not truly say that I love her enough to propose. Wisely, I let her know I was ambitious, responsibility did not fit in my agenda. Dealing that way, I suppose, was selfish, I liked having Carol around. Seeing a movie, usually, we went to a polished restaurant, but my prudent date favored wieners dipped in batter. Corn Dog Haven on Canal Street served the fried treat on a stick, and basics were pork and beans with a spicy dunking sauce.

Traipsing with Carol for nearly three years, petting gave way to sex. She let her guard down just two months before Christmas, and biding time, I liked things the way they were. Not involved with anything extraordinary, we saw the latest movies, attended dances, did a lot of fishing and enjoyed the zoo.

Vacations with our parents was fun during school years, but things changed. No one in our crowd had ever solicited the characteristics of New Orleans and with elementary things behind us, we found answers in our own back yard. On weekends, we poked into rustic places we didn't know were there. Finding facts in the French Quarter, we discovered Lafitte's Blacksmith shop, the Conti Wax Museum and the amazing Presbyter. Outstanding spires with towering steeples, the Saint Louis Cathedral is beyond imagination and stained glass windows, donated by the Spanish government inspire one's soul, without doubt, the memorable Cathedral reigns assertively in the basin of legend. Erected during the Civil War the Cabildo displays artifacts that can never be replaced, and spooking the tomb of Marie Laveau, a hodgepodge New Orleans voodoo queen, we called it a day. Looking for diversity in the town we live in, the prominent street known as Decatur has the makings of a slapstick sideshow, and as banquettes became cyclical we browsed to Broussard's.

With Christmas just six weeks away, I shopped for routine gifts planning to wrap them in my bedroom, and not fancy with bows, I did the best that I could. Hiding the loot in my closet, I know, mom would never snoop, but rummaging for soiled shirts, I covered the obvious. Finishing what I had to, I showered and shaved, crawled in bed at midnight, and lighting a cigarette, a rapid tap on my window startled me.

"Who's there?" I called. No one answered, and opening the door, Shirley stood in the doorway clothed in pink pajamas.

"What in hell are you doing here?" I glowered.

"Shhh," she muted. "Don't talk loud. You've got to come with me. I need help with Ben."

"What's wrong with Ben?" I asked.

"Come with me now, I'll explain later," she said, but I wasn't happy with that.

"Shirley, I will not budge until you tell me what's wrong."

"It's Ben, he's sprawled on the lawn in the back yard," she snarled quickly. "He's drunk. I've tried to get him upstairs, but he's out like a light."

Shirley," what in hell has happened? Is this a carry over from the rot you dished last night? I heard your foul tongue bashing Ben."

Looking at her feet, she mumbled. "We argued this evening," she said, "I didn't have supper on the table, Ben got mad, and getting drunk is nothing short of spite."

"I don't believe that Shirley. I'm sure today isn't the first time you didn't have supper on the table. Ben wouldn't get drunk over that. If he was so drunk, how did he get in the yard? Tell the truth, Shirley. What really happened?"

"I don't know," she said. "I think he fell down the stairs."

"Shirley, I've known Ben to drink, but he knows when to stop. I know you had something to do with this."

"Ben is a wimp. he won't even talk back, he walks away like a whipped puppy."

"Why do you two have words? Do you enjoy fighting? Words travel Shirley, you're the one that starts the crap."

"Maybe so and maybe not. What's he been telling you?" She snapped angrily.

"That's enough, Shirley. I can't take any more of your lies."

Putting pants on over my pajamas, I hurried to the yard, Ben was a few feet from the stairs lying on his back. Burying his hands in his stomach, he groaned miserably. Maybe he did have a few drinks, I smelled liquor, but he wasn't drunk, he was sick and getting him to his feet, he spewed miserably.

"Ohh, my stomach is sore," he groaned. "I think I'm going to pass out."

Wrapping his arm around my shoulders, by the hardest, I managed to get him upstairs. Sponging his face with cold cloths, made him comfortable, and laughing cynically, Shirley plopped on the couch.

"Just look at my noble husband," she said, "he can't even hold his liquor."

"Cut the crap, Shirley. Ben was never like this. He's not drunk, he's sick. Now, tell me what happened."

"Get that from him. You two are always up each other's ass."

I was tempted to slap the bitch, but anger and overflowing adrenaline stopped me. Defiantly, she called me every name in the book, that, I ignored and screaming like a banshee she came at me with her fists. Pushing her, maybe too roughly, she fell, hitting her head on a footstool, blood oozed, and feeling the warm trickle, she rubbed the cut and callously, licked her finger.

"Shirley, your mind is a trash bin. Ben and I are like brothers. We grew up together. Now that you've got a cut on your head can't you get it through your thick skull? Ben loves you! If you don't love him don't take him for a fool. Get out of his life!"

"Well, I'll have to tell him," she yelled, "that's something he'd like to hear."

I should not have said that. I wasn't sure if Ben was sleeping, maybe he did overhear. Staying with him throughout the night, Shirley dozed on the couch, but seeing daylight, I nudged her at 5:30.

"Shirley, Ben will feel better if he can hold something hot. Will you make a pot of coffee?

"All right, but not for him," she said, "I'll do it for you."

Giving her a crooked look, I ignored the remark, and minutes later, she brought freshly brewed coffee with two cups.

Feeling the ache i his stomach, Ben stirred restlessly and bracing himself on a pillow, he apologized.

"I'm sorry Ryan, my stomach feels hot, my insides are sore, and believe me, I'm miserable."

Holding a cold cloth at his forehead, Ben sipped the warm liquid, and not thinking too much of Shirley's attitude, I tried to understand. Why is this lovely girl so hateful, and what about this turbulent obsession with me?

Shirley stayed in the kitchen, perhaps deliberately, but I had to leave. "Ben feels better Shirley," I told her, "he's sleeping and I don't think I should move him. Sleeping on the divan for one night shouldn't be too much to tolerate."

She fumed angrily coming toward me. Her eyes glared wildly and pulling the top of her pajamas off, she shouted.

"Take a good look, Ryan. I'd be willing to bet you'd like to play with these."

Exposing her breasts was extreme. How could Ben not see? Glancing at the sick soul on the bed, Ben was in a sound sleep, and goaded with malice for the bitch that had probably caused Ben's condition, I put a coverlet over him and went home.

Ben's father was just leaving for the store when I opened my door at 6:00 o'clock. I waved, hoping that he would not encourage conversation, and getting back to Ben, I wondered what really happened. I expected he might have said something last night, but he was sick, then again, it was not likely that he would demean Shirley.

The next day, plunging into serious obligations necessary to complete three blueprints, I put last night's incident in back of my mind. The house on Paris Avenue was nearly finished. Dad had purchased the eight-room structure six month ago and after remodeling, painting was left to hired help.

Advertising in the Times Picayune, dad sold the unit within two weeks and banked a $32,000.00 dollar profit. Daniels and Son was firmly established, a stickler for perfection, dad taught all that I had to know, and I liked working with him. Knowing the fine principals of sound contracting, I worked well with hired help, but not having Ben around, all work and no play didn't cut it.

Calling Carol, I got no answer, and bored to the hilt, I planted my butt at the Black Orchid in a cloistered corner near a fish tank. Feeling left out of things, I ordered gin and tonic with a tall glass of water. I always had water between drinks, and in a state of melancholy, tonight, I intend drinking more water than usual. The music box blared, two couples were on the floor swinging to the maddened tongs of jitterbug jive, then, glancing at the couple walking through the door, I spotted Shirley wrapped around Norman Porter. Maneuvering further beyond the fish tank, I heard Norman order drinks and whatever they were talking about the guy appeared interested. Shirley seemed to enjoy letting him paw at her bosom, and sickened with the scene, I left through a back door.

Parking my car in the drive, I noticed a light in Ben's bedroom. Knowing he was alone, I decided to visit, and knocking three times, my inebriated friend finally opened the door clinging to a drink.

"For Heaven's sake Ben, try to steady your self." I said. "Why do you drink so much?"

Helping him to the couch, he plopped heavily.

"What's going on, Ben?" I asked, and slurring his words, he let me have it.

"Oh, dun't chu know? Shirley told me che wants a divorce," and pushing his finger awkwardly, into my chest, he garbled. "Che said you told her to get it."

Shirley was inclined to spread crap, but Ben had to know the truth.

"Ben, it's not by choice, but it seems I'm involved in your affairs. Please, listen. Shirley came to me last week for help. You were lying in the yard unconscious, and I'm just beginning to realize you don't know what really happened. Take stock in yourself, Ben, you're drunk now! Drinking isn't going to solve anything."

Reaching to place the glass, Ben missed the table, then running his hands through his hair, he stared at the ceiling.

"Help me, Ryan," he mumbled. "Help me to get through this. We're married just fourteen months and already, she wants a divorce. I love her Ryan, but she can't take living on my salary. I don't know what more she wants. We fight constantly, always about money. We're not paupers, Ryan," he said with a worthless shrug, "I bring home $200.00 every week, we don't pay rent and utilities are not demanding." Groaning miserably, Ben leaned on a pillow and muttered something that I could never believe.

"I have to let go, buddy. I won't hang around if she doesn't love me. It's best that we split now."

"Look, Ben," I said, "no matter what happens, all that I've said was in your defense. Some marriages just don't work. You're too nice a guy, Ben, Shirley is dragging you down, she's putting a ring in your nose."

"No, not any more, Ryan," he said, "I'm going to tell her tomorrow. If she wants out, I won't stop her."

But Shirley was with Norman Porter, she may not come home.

The next day Shirley's car was parked in the drive. She and Ben were having words and minutes later, she came downstairs carrying a suitcase. Two weeks later she filed for divorce. Ben sulked, more than he should, Shirley got what she wanted, but why would she walk? This foolish girl could not have found a more perfect husband.

Ben hit the bottle, often, he was drunk, and living with uncertainties, he was touchy.

CHAPTER SIX

Getting a few kicks from the late show, "Morgus the Magnificent" had dreamed up another idiotic scheme. Intending to melt forty pounds of weight from a woman, he put her in the oven he had invented, and with that bizarre charade, I flipped the switch. Sprawled across my bed, the phone rang, and knowing the voice at the other end, I spoke candidly.

"Hello Mr. Rollins. How are you?"

"I'm fine, Ryan," he sighed. "I'm sorry to disturb you so late, I'm calling to ask about Ben. He hasn't been home for two days. Do you happen to know where he is?"

"He's not here, Mr. Rolling," I said, "but I'll look around. I know his hang outs."

"I wish you would, Ryan, I'm terribly worried, but I don't want him to know. If you do run into him, don't tell him I called, and thanks for looking."

"I'll do my best, Mr. Rollins, Please don't worry, Ben is just a little woolgathered, don't like putting it like this, but I strongly believe Ben is feeling sorry for himself."

"You could be right, Ryan. I know how much he loved Shirley. All during the time they were married, I could see Ben was worried, but he would not confide in me and I would never meddle."

"We've talked, Mr. Rollins. Ben told me that Shirley is no longer living with her parents. She left town last week. Her mother said she was staying with a friend, she didn't put a name to the friend, but maybe Ben is looking for her. I haven't been seeing too much of him, Mr. Rollins, I've been giving him room, but I do know he's hitting the bottle. It could be he's feeling guilty, maybe he wants to be by himself for a while. "

"Perhaps that's true, Ryan, but this is not like Ben. My only hope is that I won't have to report this to the police."

"Please, don't do that just yet, Mr. Rollins. Let's check one more time. Will you meet me in the back yard with a key to the apartment?"

"Ryan, that's the first place I've looked. I've been upstairs at least five times and again today. He's not thinking straight, Ryan, I'm terribly worried."

"Humor me, sir. Let's look again." I insisted. "I'll meet you in the yard."

"All right, Ryan, maybe he is home by now. I'll get the key."

Opening the back door we smelled liquor, the room was musty, and Bed was sprawled in a disheveled bed. All that he wore, was jocks, and seeing the chaotic state of his son, Mr. Rollins propped him on a pillow seeming to understand. I hurried with a cold cloth, Mr. Rollins sponged his face, and caring as a concerned parent, he volunteered a advice.

"I've been suspecting something like this, Ben. You've been brooding too long. Why not consider something easily lost, isn't worth having." It's just two months, Shirley is probably mixed up, maybe she needs time to think."

"I'm sorry, Dad, I guess I'm a lost cause. I don't know if I can ever stop loving her."

"You need time, son, just give yourself time," and smirking a bit, Mr. Rollins asked.

"Ben. Where were you, I opened your door at least six times.

"I'm sorry dad. When I heard the key in the lock I was ashamed, I couldn't face you. I crawled under the bed hoping you would not look."

"I understand, Ben, but you must get something in your stomach. Why don't you shower? We'll go to a nice restaurant and order that lobster we've been shoving aside."

"That sounds good, dad," Ben said. "Will you come with us Ryan?"

"We'll go another time, Ben," I said, "take time now with your father, we'll get together soon."

Confiding with his father, Ben's mood was better. We saw LSU football games abd one routine Sunday, I asked him to go with me to the Quarter.

Just as Carol and I had traipsed, Ben was interested in Decatur Street. Burning time, we browsed through a hodgepodge of wax at the Conti Muse. Civil War scenes, so realistic, chilled my skin, authentic cannons, fired during the war were displayed on mock battlefields, and reaching the last tableau, we learned that world champion heavyweight John L. Sullivan and James J. Corbett had squared off on September 7th, 1892 fighting for the title on a river barge at the foot of Decatur Street. James Corbet KO'd John Sullivan, the youthful contender collected a 25,000.00 dollar purse and the bout lasted 27 rounds.

Ben was pretty much into the fight game, relating to what he had learned, the museum seemed to perk his disposition.

"Ryan, that place is interesting, I should have visited long before now. I would have enjoyed knowing the fine points of the fight game, especially, that far back."

Looking for other interests, we encountered mimes performing so realistically, one would think the character was wound with a key, and ever present, the up-side-down hat timorously, silently, urged means to a handout. Ben flipped a dollar, I, did too, and just up the street, four Negro lads tapped to rhythm that belonged strictly to them. Vagabond performers were everywhere, and ever present, the up-side-down hat, timorously, coaxed a mediocre wage.

"I'm getting hungry." Ben said. "Let's get something to eat."

Suggesting Arnauds Restaurant, my mouth was fixed for a sirloin, a stickler for seafood, Ben ordered stuffed flounder and waiting for service, Ben drank a Bloody Mary, and I had hometown Falstaff. Ben's flounder was served with buttered spinach, and strips of fried eggplant, my steak was broiled to perfection, baked potato and spinach suited me fine, and candidly, the waiter mixed Caesar salad at out table. Ironically, Ben did not mention Shirley, but listlessly pushing food to the side of his plate, evidently, he has not forgotten her. But why did Shirley drop from sight? I wondered about that.

CHAPTER SEVEN

Leaving Ben to providence, the following morning dad nudged my shoulder.

"Ryan, get up. Mother fainted this morning, she's not well, we have an appointment with Doctor Carter. Get to the office as soon as you can. I'll call the minute I know what's wrong."

I did as dad told me, but concerned about mom, my mind wondered, and finally, at 1:15 dad called.

"Ryan, your mother had a slight bout with low blood pressure, Doctor Carter has discovered borderline diabetes and before coming home, I must bring a prescription to the drugstore."

"We'll be home shortly, son. I'll explain then. If the crew comes in before 3:00 o'clock, you may as well come home. Don't look for me, I'll be with your mother the rest of the day."

When Mack checked in at 3:00, I told him that mom was sick and asking him to lock the office, I hurried home.

The ordeal seemed to drain her strength, mom was pale. Dad

Insisted she stay in bed, and plunging into dinner duty, I opened a can of pork and beans, boiled six wieners and dad was quick with a can of chicken noodle soup. I buttered six crackers, dad toted the makeshift meal to mom, and drinking something hot, mom seemed to regain spirit. it wasn't much of a meal, and far as I know, mom had never been served in bed.

Mom's rush to the doctor threw us for a loupe, and to top all, two days later, New Orleans was threatened with disaster. Hurricane warnings were never ignored at my house. Good or bad, dad practiced caution. I filled the car with gas, dad drove to the supermarket for staples, lamp oil and batteries. Filling five gallon bottles with drinking water, I stashed them in the bathtub, and for other necessities I filled the two sanitary tubs in the wash room. Under tension with a storm named Betsy, Dad tightened his brow spurting facts that I should have taken time to understand long before now.

"Ryan," he lectured, "gale winds are up to 100 miles an hour, that's the beginning of a hurricane and it's headed this way. Weathermen are wary, I don't like what I hear. This city is six feet below sea level, Lake Pontchartrain is a sheet of water 630 miles wide, twenty-five feet deep, and there's the Mississippi and gulf of Mexico. These bodies cannot be ignored. If your wasn't feeling so poorly, I'd go north to Uncle Jim in Shreveport.

Taking precaution, dad was right. Thirty-six hours later, September 9, 1965, just after midnight, the hurricane struck. Dad had mentioned strong wind velocity, and true enough, powerful gales hit with thundering roars. Windows rattled behind protective plywood, we were safe from shattering glass and keeping curiosity under the roof, we didn't dare to open a door. The entire night was scary, all that we could do was pray and hope for the best.

Sunrise told the story. Streets were flooded, however, our neighborhood was spared, and thanks to the battery operated radio, we learned Robert E. Lee Boulevard, just a few blocks from the lake , was three feet under water. Mack was hit hard, and reaching his family with a row boat, dad suggested.

"Mack, wouldn't it be best to secure your home until the water goes down? Stay with us, Sarah will be delighted having company. We were fortunate Mack, the wind let up at the right time, our house is just two blocks from the flooded area."

"Thanks, Ed. Are you sure you can handle all three of us?" Mack asked.

"The guest room is cozy, Mack, dad assured. "We haven't had company for a long time, and Mitzy will enjoy romping with your boy."

Harmony worked well at home. Six days later, when the water settled, Mack opened his door to disaster. Sand from the lake covered six rooms, furniture was hopelessly buckled, and sentient irony, two tiny crabs scurried along the kitchen wall. Jane was horrified, she cried uncontrollably and Mack had a time trying to soothe the hurt. "Don't cry, Jane, starting from scratch can be interesting and remodeling will be fun. We'll be fine."

Taking me aside, Mack said, "This is a shock for my wife, she can't cope with this now, I'll come back tomorrow and do what I can."

"That might be better," dad said, "and you can count on us. No one can do much without hardware. There's just three stores in the neighborhood that I know of and I'm sure they have been damaged."

Drinking root beer for a while, and impatient for a cold beer, dad let loose.

"Mack" he said rather irked, "I'm going to look for ice. It's been quite a while since we've had a cold beer."

But ice was hard to find. Dad was gone for two hours and dumping a fifty pound slab in the picnic cooler, he came home mad as a wet hen.

"That son-of-a-bitch," he growled. "things aren't bad enough having to do without electricity and things we take for granted, swindlers are robbing everybody. I had to pay $6.00 for this ice and it doesn't feel like fifty pounds. The bastards take advantage," but having found the slab, dad filled the glasses with ice and in spite of an unruly disposition, he popped the corks on two Regals.

Three months later, Mack and Sarah were reasonably, situated in their home. Of course there was a lot more to do, but at least, they were comfortable. Contractors were in demand, business began to adjust, dad hired two helpers, and with mom getting tired too often, dad put a stop to cooking.

Waiting in line at the "Chinese Pagoda," I was famished. Selecting Mandarin duck with fried rice, I choose fruit punch and went ahead to find a table. Clearing my tray and half caring, I looked around finding Carol with a guy I didn't know, I was shocked. She didn't see me, but the obvious motion directing my parents to where I was sitting, drew attention, She waved, and that was all there was. Food stuck in my throat, I hardly ate, and fidgeting nervously in my seat, anger seemed to bubble. Maybe I was in love, and turning to my food, taste buds were zilch. I had to know. In the privacy of my room, I called, letting the phone ring fifteen times. The call awakened logic, never realizing we were no longer teenagers, I considered Carol a prop, a buddy in jeans, never realizing she was a woman. Often, she would say, "I love you, Ryan," but immature in style, I have never realized I, am a man. I was so wrong, surely, she sensed that, and finally, I've learned.

Calling until 11:00 o'clock, Carol did not answer. Wearily plopped across my bed, my mind raced. Have I lost my girl? Heavily, attached to the scene at the restaurant I felt rejected, unmanageable vibes sickened my soul and doubt played havoc in my head. The phone rang at midnight and seeming concerned, Carol fretfully asked.

"If you want to talk, Ryan, we can drive some place to hash things. How about tomorrow?"

"Of course, Carol. I'll call for you after office hours. Is the Rockery all right? We can have dinner."

"That's fine, Ryan, I'll be waiting."

She hung the phone, and nervously, I waited for another day.

The following evening we drove the boulevard in silence. Apparently, Carol didn't know where to start, I couldn't imagine seeing her with someone else, and had a friend ratted the incident, I would not have believed. Parking at the Rockery, I walked to the opposite side of my car offering help from the low seat. Carol took my hand, and getting out of the car, she looked puzzled.

"Why, thank you, Ryan," she said smirking. "This is a first. You've never been so considerate."

That was it! A concrete foundation epitomizing my faults, she didn't have to say another word, I sensed the rest.

"Carol," I said peeved to the point of hostility, "seeing you with someone else made my blood boil. If you did it to make me jealous, it worked."

"Ryan, please don't be angry, I've been dating Robert for nearly three months. I was waiting for the right time to tell you, and now, I suppose, we must face facts. The problem is mine, but you are the blame."

Me," I said puzzled.

"Yes, Ryan," she said, "You don't want commitment."

Teary eyed, she flipped a tear with her finger, then, glaring irately, I knew she was hurt.

"Without commitment I'm not getting anywhere. I love you, Ryan, but you're using me, and I don't like being used."

"Carol," please understand, I said, "commitment goes further. I want to have something to offer a wife, without security marriage goes haywire."

"No, Ryan, it's more than that. You're thinking of Ben and what Shirley did to him. You don't trust me, or anyone."

"That's not true, Carol, Ben is not an inspiring role model, but if you want commitment I'll put a ring on your finger."

"Ha!" she laughed, "Isn't that nice? I must have bruised your ego?"

Sensing the identical sting, criticizing Shirley, Ben avoided me then, and now, Carol wants out. Steadfast with Carol, I should have been passionately romantic, and trying my damnedest to encourage passion, I kissed her. Embracing my girl, masculinity seemed to crawl from nowhere, my entire body tingled, but Carol was motionless, romantic tendrils didn't reach, and I discovered why.

My kiss had no kick, no charm to chill the blood. Call it "awakened manhood," whatever the feeling, I was possessed. Smearing her tears with my finger, I wondered, is this love, or merely, fantasized infatuation?

"My darling girl," I said, smiling, "will you marry me? I love you, Carol," and realizing another first, never before had I ever said, "darling."

"Ryan," she argued, "this is all well and good, but I want more. I'm not a lottery ticket up for grabs. I don't appreciate these whenever you want flings. You hide feeling, you hide compassion, and I don't where you stash love."

Trying to soothe an uncomfortable moment, I asked, "please let me explain," but she wasn't interested.

"I can't handle this anymore, Ryan. I've been loving you for nearly three years. I don't seem to have a future with you. We're going no where. I want a husband who will love me, I want children. That takes commitment, Ryan, and commitment if not what you want. I've been in this idiotic rut for too long, all, because I love you, but you're blind to the way I feel. That's all there is to it. I'm 23 now, I don't intend waiting much longer, I want to be with someone who loves and understands. Why is it Ryan, I've never been able to understand you?"

She was hurt, and I hurt her. Carol read through me like an open book making me realize how selfish I'd been. I suppose I did take her for granted, we were compatible in every respect, and as a result, I overlooked giving what Carol really wanted.

"Carol," I said gently, "seeing you with someone else made me realize. maybe I didn't say it, Carol, but I do love you. Could it be our matter of fact compatibility put a damper on romance?"

Challenged to a decision, I was caught off guard, but Carol stood firm.

"Let's think about it, Ryan," she said, "maybe I'm not right for you, far as I know, you haven't dated any one but me. Take time to look, Ryan, Susan Spencer has an eye for you, ask for a date, she won't turn you down."

Sarcasm, I suppose, is what I deserved, and finally, knowing what caused the split, I tried to amend.

"All right, Carol. If that's what you want, I'll miss you. but why not put this on a trial basis? You could change your mind.

"No, Ryan," she insisted, but there's nothing wrong with being friends, look at it this way. I want to play the field."

"All right, Carol, if that's what you want," but I was curious.

"You don't have to answer, but I wish you would. Are you in love with the guy I saw you with?"

"No Ryan, I don't think I am, but I like the way he treats me. When you saw us at the restaurant, that was our fifth date, he hasn't said anything definite, but I do feel solid vibes."

"Who is he? I haven't seen him around," I asked humbly.

"Of course you haven't" she said, he is Robert Frazier. His father is a CEO transferred from Birmingham to a brokerage firm on Canal Street."

Not expecting much, her attitude was curt all the way home. She hardly spoke, and if she did, I had no defense. Parking the car, I walked around to open the door and offering my hand, Carol coiled her eyes.

"Well," she said, "This is a first."

Stoked with ridicule, I compared Carol with Shirley. Both were complicated. I saw Carol wanting romance, and having a yen for money, cash was Shirley's penchant.

Never, one for romance, I'm a rugged kind of guy. Carol had a rugged side too. Managing the outdoors we enjoyed the beauty of nature, but things changed. Carol wanted love that I didn't know how to give, and why did she wait so long to tell me? Necking in my car, romance may have been slipshod, but virility was ever active. Lately, she reneged, it's been a while since we've had sex, and how long must a guy tighten his thighs?

CHAPTER EIGHT

S tarting our day, at 8:00 a.m. the next morning, dad was pleased hearing good news. The bid that he had submitted on an apartment complex was accepted. Purchasing the two-story building at a reasonable price and quite pleased with the deal, we knocked off early, and to celebrate, we drove to Jim's Chicken Inn joining Mack and the ladies.

Ordering the "special" along with a Regal beer, dad seemed to disapprove, and knowing my dad, I got the message. Letting him know about the split with Carol, perhaps like Ben, I thinks dad fiddled with the notion that I too, could be leaning towards the bottle.

"I know what you're thinking dad, but my taste buds appreciate beer with baked chicken and potato. I'm not one to cry in my soup."

"I hope not, son, but coping with a let down it's easy to get drunk. I'm not one to give advice, Ryan, but let me say this." Dad raised a brow, smirked a bit and humorously mentioned "there's more than one fish in the stream."

That night in bed, I twisted until nearly 4:00 in the morning, perhaps I had too much to eat, then again, virility cannot be ignored. Not having been with anyone for nearly a month and not thinking much of the way that Carol dumped me," the sudden break-up pulled the skids from under me. Three years without commitment, she accused, but the first two years were insipid. Carol was not serious, neither was I, and commitment was a simple peck on the cheek. I hadn't realized my affection until prom night when we were parked in front of her house. I got a little fresh, Carol wasn't too sure, and it wasn't until the second year that our relationship got cozy. Carol said "yes" to sex, and beyond that, I didn't look. I was never too aggressive, fondling with care, I enjoyed the tendrils that led to a rapturous climax. Taking Carol for granted, she seemed to enjoy what I gave, but the sudden split hit hard. I didn't bother to figure why, and as dad had encouraged, "there's more than one fish in the stream."

Thinking of our secluded hole-in-the-wall, the Black Orchard Lounge had a lot to do with growing up, we celebrated respective birthdays in that grotto and though the has fallen to the wayside, I will never forget that bubbly corner? Tim Burton, the owner, was a stickler for ID's, he didn't let us have the hard stuff until we were nineteen and the limit was two. We didn't celebrate, we talked, flushed a few off color jokes, and sipped a limited amount of beer. Togetherness was good, and now, there's nothing.

Dancing around life, it seems, Ben has lost his [ride, wearing apathy like a suit of armor, he hardly smiles, friendship is nonchalant and I don't prod. It could be, he just wants to be left alone.

Shirley has been gone for six weeks, the guy is hurt, and not knowing where she is, he might be concerned. When Carol dumped me, I walked, not with a grain of salt, but I let go. In turn, Ben, seemed to bind misfortune with misery.

Groping to encourage friendship, all that I say falls on deaf ears.

Days that followed, nothing worth while encouraged my world. Leaving well enough alone, I stretched across my bed turning to television, and having little time to unwind, mom came to my room.

"Ryan," she mentioned, "I'll be at the mall tomorrow. Do you want me to shop for you?

Bay Rum and black socks were in mind, and checking toiletries, I gave her a list.

"Mom," I mentioned, "dad wants to open the office early tomorrow. I'm glad you asked, I do need a few things. Do you have time to shop for me?"

"Of course, Ryan, it's no problem."

"Are you taking the car?" I asked.

No, Ryan. Jane wants to shop for kitchen curtains. Mack is driving us, and tonight we're to meet your father for dinner. There's left over food in the refrigerator, but I'm sure you and Ben will head to the lakefront for seafood."

"Probably so, Mom." I said.

Ben and I did have seafood, but the cool lake breeze put a kink in my neck. In bed before 10:00, o'clock, I woke with a pain in my shoulder, glancing at the clock, it read 2:35 a.m., and recognizing that redundant tap at my window I was annoyed.

Of course, it was Shirley, and before I could stop her, she egged her way into my room holding a suitcase.

"Shirley!" I bellowed, "what in hell are you doing here at this hour, and what's with the suitcase?"

"Ryan, please, I need help," she said rather exhausted. "My parents aren't home and I don't have my key. Anyway, I don't want them to know I'm back. I need a place to sleep," and quickly, she added "just for tonight, Ryan."

"You have friends," I said offensively, "why come to me? Damn you, Shirley, Ben is just across the yard."

"Yes, Ryan, I have friends, but it's late, and you're the only one I could think of. This back room is private, I don't think your parents heard when I knocked. Please, Ryan let me stay. I'll sleep on the floor and leave early in the morning."

Her eyes were teary, dark, puffy circles, hindered her looks, but why wouldn't she go to Ben? He would take her back in a minute. Sitting on the edge of my bed, she cried, but knowing Shirley's tricks, I did not weaken. regardless of circumstance, Shirley had a way looking for attention. She was never sincere and would never begin to realize the hurt she caused.

"Shirley, you might be asking innocently, but you cannot stay, if Ben knows you're here, he will never understand. Go to Ben, he'll take you back in a minute."

"No, I didn't come to start over," she said, "I have an interview at 9:00 this morning. I'm trying to find work."

"Go to a motel," I lashed.

"I don't have enough money," she said, "if you don't help me, I'll sleep in my car. It's parked outside," and raising a brow, she tormented, "maybe Ben won't notice."

That was definitely a threat, surely, Ben would notice the car that he paid for, but something wasn't right. Shirley came with a reason and sex was the gender. Staring fixedly at me, offered free reign and needing time in the sack, I didn't weigh the circumstance.

"Shirley, I don't want Ben to know you were ever here," I argued. "I'll pay for the motel."

Rolling her tongue over her lips, she hesitated. "All right Ryan, but it's late, I'm tired and I don't like driving alone on Airline Highway. Will you come with me?"

I had to get her out of my house. The Super Store opened at 7:00, Ben usually started the day, and quickly, I grabbed the suitcase.

Stopping at a Travel Lodge, she registered incognito. The clerk assigned rear lodgings and Shirley occupied room 112.

"Ryan," she asked, "will you let me have a cigarette? I'm all out."

After a few short puffs, Shirley crushed the cigarette. Grinding her hips like a stripper, she pulled me close, my groin pulsated, my heart beat rapidly, and coaxing me to the floor, I weakened. Kissing sloppily, her hand reached for the zipper in my pants and fondling generously, she got what she wanted. But sex without a condom was not my style, and rolling to the side, she was baffled.

"What's the matter?" She asked annoyed. "That weapon is ripe, Ryan. Don't you want to enjoy this?"

"Shirley," I stressed, "I don't ride bareback."

"Holy Moses," she griped, "you have amazing control, but don't fret, I carry spares."

Dumping the contents of a well equipped handbag, I noticed three Trojan skins, two Tampax pods, a full line of makeup, and a large safety pin.

"Here," she scoffed, "take your pick, yellow, pink or green."

Indicative to habitual need, expertly, she twisted the tip, delicately applying the Trogan, and smiling wickedly, her tongue encircled the channel in my ear. The glorious tingle pushed me to goad fiercely, and reaching the height of passion, I melted to a torturous moan. Coaxing me to the shower, I followed like Mary's lamb, and wanting more, I became blemished with charismatic thrills of impiety.

Shirley's hands moved with an arachnid touch, the crawling twinge blew my mind, and under the tingle of warm water, twice over, I weakened to summits of joy.

"Well," she said, looking much like the cat that swallowed the canary. "Remember, Ryan? I told you I would get to see behind that zipper? You're pretty good in the sack, my love, sex is powerful with you."

Crossing the room, she pulled a nightgown from the suitcase, and rooting for the lacy sleeves, sheer silk encircled her nakedness. Shirley lured intercourse and in a weak moment I was hooked. Lighting a cigarette from the pack that I had thrown on the table, she stretched across the bed, and not looking for further intimacy I phoned for a cab.

"Shirley," I charged, "Don't think this is going to become a habit. You wanted this, I gave what you wanted, but no more."

"I love you Ryan. All I want is to please you."

"Cut the crap, Shirley," I said, "and don't make news of this."

The cab came within minutes, and driving home, I focused regret. Hailed a brazen bitch on campus, fellows joked about the many studs that Shirley had in her closet, and judging her cynical side, the entire campus considered she was "easy."

CHAPTER NINE

The following day, I showered quickly. Hungry as a bear, I rushed to the kitchen. Dad and mom were having breakfast, and on the stove, I spotted a pot of freshly cooked grits. Reaching for a bowl, I spooned a generous portion, and adding two chunks of butter, mom was at the stove frying eggs straight up, and with dad gaping strangly, something had to be in the wind,

"What?" I asked. Dad gaped strangely over his cup, something had to be in the wind.

"What?" I asked puzzled. "Have I done something I shouldn't have?"

"Oh, no Ryan, not at all."

Dad grinned, mom giggled, and teasing like kids, they seemed to enjoy making sport of me.

"Ryan," dad said placing his cup in the saucer. "I have a proposition to offer. "I don't know how much you have in the bank, but you must have some money."

"Sure, dad. I've been saving for seven years. I have a little more than four thousand. Why do you ask?"

"That's a nice sum of money, son," he said lifting a brow. "Are you willing to invest?"

Dad had something up his sleeve and I was curious.

"Sure, dad," I said. "Do I get a raise to go with the investment?" Laughing at my own joke, and smiling with me, mom reached for my hand.

"When you hear what your father has in mind you wont have to ask for a raise. This is something much better," she assured. Dad grinned pompously, mom seemed excited and I was never more curious.

"Ryan," dad finally, explained, "I have too much in front of me. What your mother and I have in mind will take work, but there's a question. Are you willing to sink your teeth into something that will pay?"

Filling his cup, dad put it in plain words. "I'd like to turn over the apartments on Mirabeau to you. I'm sure the place can be repaired in less than a year, or maybe sooner. The building is solid, it has potential and you can charge paint and sheet rock to the business. That will get you started, the rest is up to you, and we will discuss monthly payments when the building is fully occupied."

"Think of it as a gift," mom interrupted, and winking at me slyly, she added. "Use common sense, son, accept your father's offer and you will profit nicely."

"Wow, that's a proposition all in my favor," I squealed. "Gosh, dad, do you really want me to have the building? I thought you bought it for security when you and mom retire."

"Well, I suppose I did," dad grinned, "but you're not getting anywhere too fast on a weekly salary. It's a challenge, son, but starting in your early twenties, you can make it work. I'll consider 6% interest, and a twenty-five year mortgage."

"It's worth your salt," mom said. "We've been discussing your future for some time and we're pleased knowing that you're pleased."

I think dad was rather proud offering so lucrative a future, and how lucky can a guy be? Silently, blessing my parents, I had trouble trying to check the beholding sting that burned in my eyes. The building was run down, dad had already replaced the roof, repairs would put a kink in my bank account, but counting on profit, eight units at $200.00 per unit, would easily pay the note. Essentials will come from my salary and latching to a golden opportunity, I was ecstatic. Tenants will pay $219,000.00, the original price of the building, I could do most of the work without help, but to get started, I hired three experienced carpenters. Curbing cost, dad kept me posted on short cuts, and working my butt off for eight months, I began to think like a Landlord.

Along with Daniels & Son. mom volunteered to keep my finances in order, and having to rebuild my bank account, I went back to work with dad. Seven of eight apartments were rented within four months. I worked nights trying to finish the last one and paying dad the first note, the $1,600.00 dollar receipt geared my untutored mind to think like a man.

Working steadily, Carol was never in my thoughts, but episodes with Shirley were vivid. Not having seen the girl for more than two years, strangely enough, I wondered about her.

Ben was dating now. I didn't see him too often, but understanding the guy, I imagined, something was rocking in the wind. Me, well, I'm not into dating, not just yet, Daniels & Son keeps me occupied.

Sunday rolled around portraying a favorable day. Mom and dad took in a movie, Mitzy followed me around the house seeming to want something, and assuming it might be water, I added three ice cubes to the blue Pyrex dish in the kitchen. Mitzy chewed the chunks as usual, and curbing a four hour wait before feeding her, I put three milk bones. Now, would be an ideal time to bathe the little fox, and filling the wash tub in the garage the phone rang. Of course, it was Shirley. Ironically, welcoming the call, I showered, shaved, and dressed with sonic speed.

Before parking, I scanned the lot at the Ramada Inn. Tapping lightly, Shirley answered the door wearing a black negligee, and prancing to a nearby table, she poured two drinks.

"How have you been, Ryan," she cooed sulkily, extending the glass, "it's been quite a while."

Nudity didn't bother her. Truly exquisite, her body was tanned with a silky sheen, her hair glistened, and touched with copper, her eyes sparkled. Her lips were so vivaciously curved, with little effort, this licentious female could make a man melt. It wasn't like that with Carol, I have never looked upon her naked, the slight mark at the back of her neck is not noticeable, but with Shirley, I haven't seen a blemish.

Catering to rancid standards, sex is the name of the game, and foreplay is sweet. Shirley is not just sexy, she is a banshee entwined with bizarre, adventurous sex. Entranced with the immoral bitch, I cannot determine whether I like or resent her. Liquor seemed to stir virility, three exotic spasms blew my mind, each time, Shirley gave more.

"Ryan, my darling, I love you. I want to make you happy, I'll never let you go."

"Shirley, I don't like that kind of talk, you've been away a long time. I don't love you and never will. A bottle of whisky, the handy ice bucket and the negligee act doesn't fool me. I'll go along with these impetuous schemes, just remember, you're chasing me."

The girl was weird, eccentric, and far out, but weaned from Carol, I was led to a pastures generating a brand of sex that curled my toes.

"Ryan, my divorce is final. I'm not obligated to Ben and neither are you. I thought I loved Ben, but deep down, I never did. Would you want to stay with a woman you don't love?"

"I don't know the answer to that, Shirley," I said. "No two people can tie the knot and be positive about anything. But you've been away. Where in hell did you go"?

"No place in particular, Ryan. but aren't you glad I'm here?"

Avoiding the question, I said. "Shirley, I don't want to discuss Ben, marriage or love. I have to go now."

Sprawled across the bed, Shirley was out like a light. Booze had a lot to do with that, and hearing the cab, I threw a sheet over her and on the way out, I locked the door.

Twenty minutes later, I parked in my drive. Mom was in the garage with Mitzy, and tapping the horn, my pet ran to me wagging her tail. Petting my pooch, and ruffling her fur, I noticed silky undergrowth.

"Mom," I said, "Mitzy is in full coat."

"Your father mentioned that this morning, Ryan, but she does need a bath. Will you have time to do that? There's a fresh bar of tar soap in the laundry room."

"Sure, Mom. I intended doing that earlier, but got sidetracked."

Mitzy enjoyed the warm water, pampering her coat with a brush she licked my hand. My lovable pet was a mixture of Fox and Spitz, she slept in my room and jumped in my bed when the alarm rang. Dad enjoyed her amiable outlook and praising puppy dog wisdom, he often said, "our little mixed breed is gifted with more intelligence than a polished pedigree."

Having that second affair, I was disturbed, but Shirley called me, not pursuing her, I considered myself blameless. Behind closed doors, the rendezvous meant nothing, I played her game taking advantage of pleasure, and in Ben's company, pretense, is quite a strain.

CHAPTER TEN

Three weeks later, bumping into Ben and his date at the mall, I could not remember her name. Ben waved and walking toward the pair, Iproaching the pair, I met them half-way.

"Hi, Ryan," he said, offering his hand. "I'm sure you remember Hazel McCoy."

"Of course I remember," I mentioned uneasily, "Hazel, it's nice seeing you again." Steered from discomfort, and not seeing Ben too recently, I felt an apology was due.

"I'm sorry Ben, I should have been in touch long before now, but renovating the apartments, my social life hasn't been too active,"

"Ryan, don't apologize," Ben said. "I wish you the best of luck, that building is going to play a big part in your future. Kissing the tip of Hazel's nose, he smiled glibly. "Hazel, my friend is getting to be a workaholic. I'm glad we bumped into one another, Ryan, I've asked Hazel to marry me and want you to be the first to know, I haven't even told dad. We plan redecorating the apartment but taking time to enjoy Christmas and welcome the New Year is a first."

Ben, I wish you the best and loads of good fortune to you both."

Hazel beamed admiringly, and addressing me, he said. "Ryan, it's my turn to make decisions. Will you stand up for me?"

"Of course, Ben. I'll look forward to that honor," and kissing Hazel. I said, "Lady, you're getting a great guy!"

"Thank you, Ryan," she said, "Ben is wonderful, he knows I love him."

"Well, let's celebrate." Why not go to the Black Orchard?"

"That sounds like a winner," Ben agreed. enthusiastically. "We can go now."

Celebrating with champagne, Hazel's plans made sense, camaraderie was like old times and getting to know Hazel, I got the idea she was right for Ben. Glancing at his watch, Ben was probably aware of responsibility, holding Hazel's hand he sighed happily and staring at her with cow-eyes, Ben was in love.

"Ryan, tomorrow's centerfold is crammed with sale items, I have to open the store at 7:00. I'm sorry we have to go, but there's always tomorrow."

"Pressing my hand to his, Ben looked solemn. "Ryan, I'm glad we've had a second chance, life is much better having good friends, and thanks for the champagne."

"That goes for me too, Ben. I've enjoyed the evening. We should do this again, and Ben" I whispered, "you're getting a swell girl."

"That, I do know, Ryan. Stay in touch," he said smiling. "From now on, I'm a new man."

Within a year, my apartment building was filled. The one apartment that was not finished, I used as a personal retreat, and needing an office, I bought a desk and file cabinet. Having no problem paying dad, surely, I could support a wife, and to organize my life, I must get away from Shirley, togetherness with Ben, had discolored my irrepressible trance. Shirley has to go.

My phone rang at 10:00 o'clock, and thinking it could be Shirley, hesitantly, I answered.

"Hello Ryan," she said, chortling like a dove. "I want to talk seriously with you."

"Seriously, Shirley? How seriously?" I said annoyed.

"Oh, don't be so suspicious, Ryan," she said, "my rent's been raised. It's more than I can afford and the apartment you have empty is ideal."

The remark bothered me. Having Shirley in my building I would be a sitting duck for gossip.

"Shirley," I grumbled, "that will be like advertising a going affair. I can't do that."

"Can't or won't, Ryan? It's time to pay," she demanded, "we've been more than intimate for six months. Put me under that roof or pay for favors."

The threat riled me.

"Shirley, you call me, I do the favors, remember? Let's just call it quits."

"It's not that easy, Ryan," she threatened. "I'll be leaving to visit a friend in Hammond, and when I come back you could be in a load of trouble."

The split with Carol seemed to hamper my senses. I had no interest in the available nurse, and with Shirley, I was vulnerable. She knew how to tease. Flashing her breast encouraged the come on, and foolishly, I let it happen.

"Don't call anymore, Shirley, it's over. I don't care if I ever see you!

Slamming the receiver, I thought of Carol, she was married a little over a year, and accidentally bumping into Fred at a gas station, I learned that she was the mother of a little girl.

It was hell trying to sleep. Clasping my hands at the back of my head, seriously, I thought of my future. I liked working. Not only that, I considered myself fortunate being with dad in a thriving business, but why do I broaden this strange phobia I have towards marriage? Not able to muster love, I considered sex the alternate. Carol had it right, where did I stash love? I've never experienced the kind of sex that awakens love. I get hot and bothered, I'm sure everyone does, and to encourage my unsettled mind I turned to the dictionary.

Digging into the nitty-gritty, love can be a noun, an adjective, a verb, and with consistent variations, love has a purpose, a hope, a crave, an idea sheathing many things, but what kind of love is the secret to commitment? Carol may have loved me, but I wasn't sure of anything. Considering she was not able to unravel my uncertainty, she walked, and when that happened, I wondered. Did Ben really love Shirley?

Working with mixed emotion, my head hurt, and noticing my sluggish stride at the office, dad asked if I was sick. Maybe I was, it isn't easy being unsettled. I criticized my work, lost patience at the drop of a hat, and often, thought of Ben. Seemingly, he was crazed with a love that made him sick, and primed for a second marriage, can recoil be the answer? Another thing, Shirley had me worried. Why would a trip to Hammond make me change my mind? I can not imagine, and tacking the last piece of sheet rock, unconsciously, I gathered my tools anxious to drink something cold.

Popping the cap on a Delaware Punch, I ran into Carol at a Pick-a-Pack store on the way home.

"Hello, Ryan," she said hastily, "we haven't seen each other for quite some time. How are you?"

"I'm fine, Carol." I said. "It's nice seeing you. Fred told me about your little girl. You look great!"

"Nice of you to say," Ryan. Are you still avoiding the opposite sex?" I thought by now, you might be married."

Not appreciating trite, conversation was a bit awkward, impish tête-à-tête could very well become scathing and quickly managing the dig, I snapped.

"You're analyzing Carol, I scoffed. "Well enough should be left alone, and with a bitter taste in my mouth, I walked away.

CHAPTER ELEVEN

Reading the Steinbeck novel that I had started months before, the book was of no interest. Feeling queasy, I went downstairs, brewed a large cup of tea, and buttering crackers, doubt, crowded my mind. Have I really seen the last of Shirley?

Bored and uneasy, I watched the late movie, but contrary to what I had expected, the flick was from the early thirties. "Morgus the Magnificent" was more than I could take. Having to convince a woman she could lose weight crawling into an oven that he invented, the ludicrous farce blew my mind. Lighting a cigarette, I tried to relax and reaching for the evening paper I was interrupted by a knock at my window.

Seeing Shirley again, I was mad, she too seemed angry, and before knowing, her temper raged.

"We have to talk, Ryan," she demanded.

"Shirley, I don't know what you're up to. It's late. Why are you here? I hope you didn't wake my parents. Please Shirley, don't start anything."

"What I have to say is urgent, Ryan, you have to listen."

"All right, Shirley, I can see there's no putting you off. We'll go where we can talk," and thoroughly, irked, I drove wildly, to the lot at the Rockery.

"Shirley," I said angrily, "don't come to my house again! I've told you before, I want out! Please, just leave me alone."

"I can't leave you alone Ryan," she charged. "I'm carrying your baby. The doctor in Hammond said I'm approximately, ten weeks pregnant."

Looking fiercely into my face, she charged, "Ryan, it's true, this child belongs to you."

"Shirley," I answered pissed. "Do you want revenge that bad? I've always been carefu and how many times have you been with others? I donn't believe that."?"

"Yes, Ryan, because it's true. The others, as you put it, meant nothing to me!"

Whimpering childlike, she pulled at my clothes, and falling to her knees she yelled.

"I love you, Ryan! Don't you get it? We've been having sex for six months. I want to have your baby."

Just as Shirley had given sex, she shackled me with unbridled love. But why me? I've never encouraged love. I gave what she wanted, and too angry to say much, I pictured chaos to come. True, Shirley was sexy, she flaunted sex, and foolishly in line with the rest, she pegged me her patsy. I was just beginning to get ahead saving money from my salary, and for nearly a year, I had no trouble paying dad.

"It's true, Ryan, she whined. "I'm not lying. Help me through this, marry me and when our child is born you can have a divorce. Think about it Ryan. I can make you the most talked about patsy in the neighborhood, and don't think I wont."

You can't prove anything, Shirley. If you're in trouble your best bet is abortion."

"I've thought of that Ryan, but not your baby. I love you too much. Sure, I've been with others, but that first time with you, made me realize I love you too much to lose you, I applied the Trogan because I puncture it Ryan. It took a while, and now that I'm pregnant nothing will stop me. You will father your child!"

Seriously, giving thought to the many affairs, maybe she is telling the truth. Meeting her unexpectedly, around campus, always, she stared at my thighs, I suppose, thinking of prowess between my legs, the look invited sex, and foolishly, I tangled with a girl having the reputation of a tramp.

"I don't care how you do it,' she charged, but make plans. You turned on me, Ryan, come what may, we will be married. You and your child belong to me."

Thinking of the many times that I had willingly related to passion, there was no way to upgrade stupidity. I must have been crazy, Shirley was not the kind of girl I wanted for a wife. surely, she would never be a desirable daughter-in-law and what is she capable of?"

Considering my parents, I didn't want disgrace, and having no choice, I leaned towards possibilities.

"All right, Shirley, I'll marry you but the minute your child is born, I will file for divorce. Your baby will have my name, but marriage will cost, no more sex, and I make the rules!"

"I'll do what you want Ryan," she said wistfully.

"Every man wants a son. If I give you a son, you might change your mind." Angrily smirking, simply, she walked away.

The next evening at supper, food stuck in my throat, dad went to the den taking the evening paper, and having to discuss the jam I was in, I lagged to help mom in the kitchen.

"I'll stack the dishwasher mom," I said, and gearing to what might cause a kick in the teeth, I faced facts.

"Mom, before dad gets wind of this, can we talk?"

Mom always understood, dad would too, but I needed mom to cushion the jolt that could very well upset my father. He had faith in me, I've always known that, but confronted with a situation, faith could very well take a back seat. Bound to an indolent marriage, I needed mom.

"Mom, you and dad don't deserve this, but it's done. Please, try to understand. I'm going to be married mom, and my girl is pregnant. We didn't plan it like this, but it happened. Will you come with me when I tell dad?"

And hence, it came. No outburst, no conflict, no hostility, merely, a soft question.

"Ryan, does your girl know how many weeks she's into pregnancy?"

"The doctor said approximately, ten weeks, mom."

Burdened with mental strain, I talked fast, but mom was not fooled.

"You must love her very much," she said staring at me quizzically.

"Yes, mom, I do." Blurting the lie, deception might be a way to warmth, and recalling the look of reprieve, I remembered tearing my best trousers climbing the page fence in our back yard.

"Ryan," mom said optimistically. "Don't go into detail with your father, let well enough alone. Just tell him you're getting married and pregnancy will take care of itself. I'll come to the parlor, when I finish the dishes, I'll be with you, and Ryan, please," mom said rather sharply, "show a little enthusiasm."

Saving the supper dishes, mom seemed to hesitate. "Sit down, Ryan, she said pulling a chair from under the table. "This is all too unexpected. I don't think you're telling me the whole story. If you're in trouble, isn't it right that I know?"

Fooling mom was not a habit. Gifted with perception she never failed to recognize a grungy excuse.

"Mom, I know I've been foolish, maybe I am in love. I don't really know. I've never understood love."

Shirley had the upper hand. Clinging to the walls of hell, she hoarded a chalet of animosity, explaining in detail would make matters worse, and why encourage doubt?

"The baby is mine, mom, I've accepted that and will be responsible. I just want to get through this without humiliating you and dad."

"I understand, Ryan. Of course, you'll speak with her parents, but confide in her first. Hide pregnancy, premature birth should not be a problem and we'll plan something nice.

"That's out, mom. We don't want any thing fancy. We're going to be married by a Justice of Peace. We're satisfied with that, but there's a cog in the wheel," and hesitant, I mumbled. "It's Shirley, mom, Ben's ex-wife."

Mom did not budge.

"I know, Ryan," she said, looking over her eyeglasses. "I heard the commotion."

November 19, 1966, I married Shirley, and with nary a blink, Ben offered good wishes. Ben married Hazel three weeks later and as he had honored me, I stood proudly at his side valuing the closeness that had gone astray.

To my surprise, Shirley handled herself like a lady. She decorated the apartment, recipes taken from Good Housekeeping magazines chartered her towards the pots, and routinely, she cleaned the apartment. Often, she cuddled, but badgered with resentment, I could not warm to her. Duped into marriage, I was angry, and to avoid cold showers I turned to the friendly nurse that Fred knew. Sleeping alone, Shirley bitched, that didn't bother me, but copulating with a pregnant woman, carrying a child that may never know his true father, didn't cut it.

The inevitable came when, sympathetically, Shirley placed my hand to her stomach, her flesh bubbled with life, and feeling the forceful jolt, this unborn child could very well belong to me.

Living as siblings, Shirley dealt with the unusual. June 20, 1967, a healthy little boy came into our lives. Falsifying her period, premature birth was taken for granted, and as luck would have it, Shirley's parents were out of town. Praising grandfathers the we named the child Edward Franklin Daniels.

Shirley said she loved me, I've always believed she did, but with resentment stewing in my gut, I will not play hypocrite. Seeing my face in this child, I did not relinquish doubt, and in my heart, the child is drawn to my soul.

Giving her credit, Shirley was a good mother. Pampering Edward, she showed decency, the apartment was neat, supper was on the table when I came home, but living with knots in my stomach, I hated the bitch. Loving Edward, I could not abide his mother. I didn't want marriage, not this soon and not this way, but Edward is the key. Will Shirley tolerate living without sex because of her son, or will this vindictive girl agree to a divorce?

At three weeks, Ben and Hazel claimed Edward their godson. Rituals took place at Saint Mary's church, and after, we went home to celebrate. Mom had managed a brief get together, and in my gut, I'm sure Ben was uncomfortable, and what does he think of me? Edward slept the entire evening, and before leaving, Mack's wife, asked if his eyes were blue.

I can't say things were kosher, the stagnate routine continued for six months and Shirley has never mentioned divorce. Relaxing on the couch, she wriggled close. Looking for love, her eyes seemed to plead, but I was cool. Call it pride, perhaps spite is the better word, but living with rules, Shirley is restless. I will not be two-faced, that's what I meant when I said marriage would cost. Shirley is a stickler for sex, and the only hard she gets from me is contemptuous animosity. I don't think my mom was ever fooled, opinionated perhaps, but she has never pried, and far as I know, dad is still in the dark. Divorce is inevitable, I just don't know how or when it will happen, but I do know Shirley is irritated.

"Ryan," she growled, "This idiocy has been going on for six months. You loved me before, my darling, why can't you love me now? Search your soul, Ryan, please, stop hating me. You'll never find peace if you don't let go. I don't know what to expect anymore."

"I have never loved you, Shirley. All I want from you is a divorce. I want you out of my life! Love, huh! That never happened, it was sex, we had sex. That's all! Divorce me Shirley, tell your lawyer whatever you want, you'll get a reasonable settlement, and Edward stays with me!"

"Ryan, rest assured, I will decide," and retreating to the bedroom, she slammed the door.

The following day, work was not strenuous, but mitering is a task. Mack was involved with the two men that dad had hired after the hurricane, and the bid that dad submitted for repairs at Saint Rock drug store came through.

Two apartments on Robert E. Lee Boulevard kept us busy. With Jack Prichard knowing his way around tight seams, we hung sheet rock in four rooms. Two days later, we lowering two ceilings in a building on Claiborne Avenue, and to top all, I sipped from the fourth rung of a ladder. My back was sore for three days, my work was sluggish, lack of sleep hastened a bluish puff under my eyes, and when dad told me to order twenty pounds of eight-penny nails, I forgot.

"What's wrong, son?" Do you have a problem? Would you like to talk or should I mind my own business?"

"I'm fine, dad, bouncing Edward on my knee aggravated the pain in my back, I'm a little off key. That little guy has more energy than ants at a picnic."

But that was not the case. I was miserable making Shirley miserable. I don't suppose that makes sense, but it's true. We're two malicious individuals tearing each other apart, Shirley pests me for sex and I'm in an uproar wanting a divorce.

CHAPTER TWELVE

Leaving the office at 8:20, mom's car was parked in the drive when I reached home, Shirley's car was no place in sight, and getting the idea that Edward might be sick, I figured she was on an errand to the drug store. Finding mom resting with her head over her arms at the kitchen table, something had to be wrong.

"What's the matter, mom? Why are you here so late? Where's Shirley?"

Mom was a little put out, I've never seen her that way, but dad was in the habit having supper at 7:00 o'clock, and not being home, she was upset.

"I've been here since 11:00 o'clock, Ryan. Shirley called telling me she had to see the dentist. She's been gone all day, she hasn't called and didn't tell me who the dentist was. I called your father, he knows I'm here, but I'd like to get home. I didn't think Shirley would be this late," and aware of the strange situation, mom suspiciously mentioned, "Ryan, I wouldn't say anything about this to anyone, not just yet."

"I won't mom. When I saw your car, I thought Edward was sick. Thanks for coming. I know that dad doesn't like eating alone. I'm sorry about this, mom, you should go now, when Shirley gets home, I'll let you know."

"I didn't know where Shirley kept the baby food, Ryan, I didn't find any in the locker but there was a can of applesauce. I mashed a potato and soft-boiled an egg. Edward ate good, he should sleep through the night."

Mom left the apartment during a light drizzle, Edward, was asleep and covering him snugly, I pulled the shade down to the sill.

Popping the cap on a Regal, I relaxed, ten minutes later, I had a quick shower, and feeling whipped, I crawled into bed. The hamburger I had for lunch was enough, I wasn't hungry, just mad. Glancing at the clock, I wondered where in hell did Shirley go? Calling mom at 11:00 this morning, Shirley was gone for fifteen hours. It rained buckets, lightning cracked at random, and with streets pitch black, I figured she may not be home at all. Striking a match to light candles, Edward cried. The deafening bolt frightened him, and cuddling the little guy, I walked the floor with him until he fell asleep.

Checking the closet, the rack was rather empty, and not finding Shirley's large suitcase, I figured she had no intention coming home. I really didn't care, but thinking of Edward, I cared about him. With dad depending on me, I had to work, and not expecting my diabetic mom to care for an active child of six months, I needed help.

The following morning I phoned mom.

"Shirley didn't come home mom," I said, and hearing the phone click, she was at the apartment within minutes.

"Mom. I said baffled, "we have to talk."

"I know, Ryan. That's why I'm here."

Spreading jars of baby food, oatmeal, milk, eggs and potatoes on the table, she said. "I could not find baby food, to be sure, I stopped at the store last night. Do you have any idea what Shirley is up to?" She asked.

"No, mom, I don't. She hasn't called, but I'm sure you know what's gong on."

"Ryan, I only know what you've told me. You said you loved Shirley, I have never believed that, and what am I to think now? I've seen a lot of restlessness in this house, and you Ryan, you're loaded with tension. You're both like cats on a hot tin roof. That's no way to live, son, and you'd better start thinking. It could be that Shirley has decided to leave and don't think she won't be back for her son."

"Let's talk over a cup of coffee, mom. I called dad, he knows I'll be late, but he doesn't know about Shirley. I'll wait another day. I don't have the slightest idea what Shirley is up to. I don't even know how I should handle things, but I've got to get this off my chest."

"Ryan," mom said, locking her eyes with mine. something was bothering her too, and pouring a second cup pf coffee, she cornered me.

"Look at me, son," she said, "I love you, I love my grandson, but there's a cat in the sack. From the beginning, I didn't want to see you marry, and now, something tells me you were obligated. I'm surprised the arrangement lasted this long."

"Mom, there are things you don't know. For you to understand, I'll have to start from the beginning. You've been my consulate, mom, the truth isn't pretty, but I need your help."

"For six months, Ryan, I've been troubled. Shirley has been standoffish, I have never been able to gain her confidence, and seeming a bit superior, she said what was true.

"I'm prying, I know, but there are times when talking clears a way to sensible decisions. I'll explain to your father if you want," and grinning over her glasses she assured, "he's not the ogre you think."

"O.K, Mom, but what I have to say, I don't think dad will take with a grain of salt, and hearing the whole story, *you,* might peg me the ogre."

Hesitantly, I glanced at mom thinking of the many times I had spread my favorite treat on a slice of bread just before supper. even washing the knife and wiping my face clean, mom knew I was in the peanut butter. My parents are two of a kind, but with dad working all the time, I brought my woes to mom.

"Ryan, why are you looking at me so anxiously? Are you sure you're all right?"

"I'm humiliated, mom. What I have to say isn't pleasant."

"You're my son Ryan," she said, "say whatever is in your heart," and seeing her nod so genuinely, I let loose.

"Mom, after Shirley left Ben, late, one night, she came to my back door. I messed with her for a while, but please understand, Shirley is a girl that's been around, she knows the ropes, I just didn't count on her falling in love with me. I was cautious, that's the truth, but without my knowing, she punctured the Trogan. That girl scares me, I don't know what she'll do next."

My mother listened, said nothing, and weighing the situation, her opinion was poles apart from mine.

"Mom," I admitted, "Shirley is a sex-pot, the one way I could use authority was to stay at a distance, I have never slept with her, our marriage is in name only. It's been six months now, and knowing Shirley, she's frustrated."

"Ryan, I can imagine animosity, but never, spite. Two wrongs can never make a right. The two of you should have talked. Now, what are you going to do about Edward?"

"I'll worry about that when I see Shirley. I've tried talking, but she would never listen. If I don't hear from her soon, I'll talk to a lawyer."

Probably, Shirley was gone for good, but I couldn't expect mom to care for Edward on a steady basis.

"Mom, I asked, "I'm going to look for someone to care for Edward. Will you help? Your judgment is better than mine."

"Of course, son. I'll care for Edward while we're looking. I'll take him with me now, you can bring his crib tonight, but aren't you planing a little too soon?"

"No harm can come from hiring a nanny," I said, "if Shirley does come home, having a nanny around might make things better."

After three days, still, no word from Shirley. Dad depends on mom, I do too, but a six month grandson, that's a lot to handle. Discussed a live in, I wanted a reliable middle aged woman primarily, to cook, attend Edward and do a little washing. Allowing space for a third party, I gave the tenant next to me a month's notice. What Shirley has in mind, I don't know, maybe she will come home, and one way or another, I will not tell her parents, not yet.

Choosing the apartment next to mine, the tenant vacated two days after getting notice, and taking advantage of time, I cut a door joining the two units, repairs were finished one week later, and thinking that three comfortable rooms might appeal to someone, mom placed an ad in the weekend edition of the Times Picayune.

Struggling with the longest two days of my life, I had little sleep, and thanks to Heaven, the phone rang at 9:30 Monday morning.

"Ryan," mom said, exuberantly. "There's a lady here, she wants to meet you. Can you come now?"

Seeming to think the woman was a gem, mom briefed me in the kitchen. Meeting the potential nanny, I faced a middle-aged woman that shook my hand with the gusto of a marine, gray strands at the sides of her face, added a depth of dignity and harmoniously blended to the likes of Mother Hubbard, she was plump, the faint hint of cologne was nice, and scanning through what seemed ideal references I, was impressed.

"I'm Mildred Monahan, "Millie" for short," she grinned. "I didn't mention age on my references, but last month I've turned forty."

Millie Monahan had a certain glow, I liked her attitude, and quickly pouncing on a question that seemed important, she asked.

"Am I to understand the ad offers live-in quarters?"

"Yes," I said, "if you would like, I'll show you the apartment now. There are three rooms, a bathroom, and a small yard."

"I'd like that, Mr. Daniels. I don't have much furniture, but I'd like to see what I need and picture what I have to place."

Ginger, the girl that cleaned our house, had given the place a good going over, eight rooms were spick and span, Mrs. Monahan seemed enthused, and in the kitchen, I explained.

"You might want to try for a week or so, Mrs. Monahan, explore as you like. You will have privacy. I leave at 8:30, and if you wouldn't mind, I'd like a bit of breakfast."

Considering salary, I offered $200.00 monthly with utilities paid, and groceries were my responsibility.

Wiping a modest tear, the woman appeared relieved, and not knowing how to handle the reaction, I wished that mom had come with me.

"Mr. Daniels," she said, dabbing her eyes, "you don't know what this means. I haven't had a place of my own since my husband died seven years ago. Living with my sister, I've been running from one place to another trying to pay my way. I've been on busses and streetcars nearly every day trying to find reasonable lodging. This apartment is the best thing that has ever happened. I love children, Mr. Daniels. I'm going to enjoy taking care of your son, but there's something that I haven't told you or your mother."

What, now? I thought. Mom seemed to regard the woman a gem, but is she real?

"Mrs. Monahan, be honest with me. You seem trustworthy, but if you're in trouble, please tell me. I'll help if I can."

"Oh, no, Mr. Daniels, it's nothing like that," she smiled timidly. "I have a daughter living in Texas, Andrea works for a lawyer, she likes to visit during Christmas. I just want to ask if she can stay here with me.

"Good Heavens! I thought you were going to say something drastic," I said, "make your own decisions, Mrs. Monahan. I will respect your privacy and that of your daughter."

"It will take a little time, Mr. Daniels," I suppose for the two of us," she said. "If you won't mind, I would like to have the baby's crib in my room. I'm a light sleeper, I'll hear your little boy when he needs me."

The next day I went with the truck and two part time men to tote Mrs. Monahan's belongings. Bedroom furniture was all that she had, and with hired help, she arranged her belongings. Seeming to like the green carpet I had replaced, I knew why when she took a green bedspread from a box that had been previously packed. Making use of a rod left by the former tenant, she tailored the window with drapes that matched the bedspread and placing what seemed to be trinkets from the past on her dresser, the room improved nicely. Admiring her belongings, all neatly placed, she smiled.

"Now," she said, "all I need are three nice scarves."

Liking her attitude, I gave her two sets of keys, smiling graciously she seemed pleased, and leaving the apartment, she said.

"I'm so relieved, Mr. Daniels, my only hope now, is to please you."

Two weeks later, still no word from Shirley. Mrs. Monahan had things well under control. She organized Edward's clothing, shopped with mom for baby food and necessities, and often remarked how much she enjoyed the apartment. A whiz at cooking, Mrs. Monahan put tasty casseroles on the table, even mom had to admit, dishes that she put together weren't better. The woman was dedicated, she and Edward hit it off like relatives. Edward was never without clean clothes, he hardly cried, and when he did, Mrs. Monahan practiced wisdom that I had never realized.

When Edward was out of source, she greased the end of a thermometer with Vaseline and testing in his rectum for fever, I asked why?

"Mr. Daniels," she said smiling, "babies cry with tummy aches, other than gastric disorders intestinal fever is usually the cause, but that's on the inside, foreheads don't get hot, and I always say, it's best to be safe, than sorry."

The remark led me to believe how dedicated this woman really was, and bound to the impression, I ignored the stress of protocol.

"Mrs. Monahan, let's make things easy," I said, "please, call me Ryan."

"I'd like that Ryan. Will you accept me as Millie?"

CHAPTER THIRTEEN

"Good morning, Millie," I said, reaching for a cup. Pushing the kitchen curtains aside, I opened the window. Yesterday's downpour, had darkened the day, and today, it was nice to see the sun.

"It's going to be a good day, Millie. I peeked at Edward, would you believe, the little guy was smiling in his sleep?"

"Ahh," Millie related with a grin, "some, have the notion if babies smile in their sleep, the little ones are having angelic dreams. I tucked Edward under the covers at 8:30 last night. Your little boy slumbers sound, Ryan, he doesn't wake when I change his diaper."

Millie served two fried eggs, straight up, bacon with toast, and as yet, she hasn't shared the table, maybe she is shy, or perhaps, doesn't want to become basic. I wouldn't mind, of course, but traveling two miles to work, as Millie may have considered, I don't have time to dally. Before leaving, I peeked in on Edward. Most of the time the little guy slept with his fists clenched at the sides of his face, and snugly tucked in his crib, I envisioned a lamb cuddled in soft down. The child brings meaning to my life, but I can not rid the blistering revulsion I feel for his mother.

Six months with Millie around, worked well, she's family now, and next week Edward will celebrate his first birthday. My parents visited their grandchild often, and not hearing from Shirley, I decided to visit with her mother.

Mrs. Freeman let me in, but with eyes coiled. Maybe she was irritated, but no one was more pissed than I.

"What's going on, Mrs. Freeman? I asked. As a parent you haven't volunteered much. Where is Shirley? It's been four months since she left. You must know something by now."

"My husband is in Chicago, Ryan, we haven't discussed Shirley. I'll tell you this, but please, keep it quiet."

"Why, Mrs. Freeman? Is it that terrible?" I snapped.

"When you hear, decide for yourself," she sighed, "this is not the first time, Ryan. Shirley pulled this stunt when she was fourteen. She stayed away for nine days and until today, we don't know why. We've reported her missing twice since, the police didn't take interest then, and she was gone for nearly a month."

"Why didn't you tell me this before, Mrs. Freeman?" I demanded.

"Ryan, we've had problems. Shirley's been difficult since she was a child, she's been under psychiatric care for nearly three years. We thought marriage would make a difference, settle her behavior, but it's happening again. Ryan, she loves you more than you realize, we didn't mean to deceive you, probably, she will come home, but whatever you decide, I hope it's for the better."

"Mrs. Freeman, are you telling me that Shirley is paranoid?"

"Ryan, that's not a word we like to hear," she said curtly, "we believe Shirley is impulsive."

"Deserting her child, Mrs. Freeman, is more than impulsive. What am I supposed to do?"

"Ryan, I'm not going to pry, but my mind tells me that Shirley is doing this because something happened between the two of you. I pray she will come home. Please, Ryan, help her, she needs you."

"Mrs. Freeman, I don't care if I ever see her again, all I want is a divorce. If she does come back, I don't want her in my house."

"Ryan," Mrs. Freeman explained. "Shirley creates her own trouble. She's twenty-three now, that's old enough to know better, but she's out of our jurisdiction. Psychiatry hasn't helped, I should have told you, but if I had, you would not have married her."

"That remark tells me you wanted to get rid of your daughter, that's callous Mrs. Freeman. She may be insecure, but I will not be a patsy."

Angered, I left. More now than ever, I had to talk with mom, taking her into confidence, I told all that happened confronting Shirley's mother.

"Ryan," she said, "why not place an ad in the paper, the confidential column might help. If she doesn't want to come home, ask her to call."

"Thanks mom. I'll do that, I just hope Shirley sees it."

Millie Monahan was a godsend, and with mom's many visits, Edward enjoyed two-fold attention.

Two weeks flew like a bird on wing. I haven't heard from Shirley, nor, have I discussed her. Millie knows nothing of our estranged marriage and she hasn't asked. I didn't know the situation with Shirley's parents, with her father away, her mother didn't seem too concerned, and I got the idea they didn't care.

Having eaten spinach and stewed chicken from the Gerber menu, Edward enjoyed mashed peaches. Downing five ounces of warm milk, he fell asleep and with Millie watching television in the privacy of her apartment, I took advantage of serenity. Planning last minute changes for the St. Roch Drug Store. I spread blue prints, lit a cigarette and reaching for an ash tray the doorknob rattled. Not having changed the locks, I assumed it was Shirley, and before gathering my wit, she pranced brazenly into the kitchen.

"Well," she said contemptuously, "I'm back."

Totally unprepared for the unexpected, I sneered. "If you're here to explain, you're months too late. Your parents are looking for you. Go home, Shirley!"

"I should say not!" she shouted. "I'm staying here with my family."

"Shirley," I said soberly, "I've filed for divorce, claiming desertion, and now that you're back, I don't want you in this house."

"I know you don't want me!" she argued. "You never did! If you want a divorce, you'll have to put up with me. That's the ultimatum, Ryan, take or leave it."

Bellowing the outburst, she hurried to her bedroom slamming the door. I could jump the lock, of course, but what good would that do? We would probably argue, and the last thing I wanted was to embarrass Millie. The situation was bound to get messy, thinking how I should handle chaos, the night seemed to fly, and having no inkling of dawn, Millie ambled to the kitchen.

"Good morning, Millie," I said casually.

"Good morning, Ryan," she nonchalantly murmured.

Obviously, perplexed, I had to open up. Millie should know what is happening under the roof she considers home.

After the ruckus with Shirley, I accomplished nothing. Getting the blueprints in order, I showered, shaved, brushed my teeth, and returned to the kitchen, Millie had filled two cups with hot coffee, Edward was probably sleeping, that worked well, and fusing this serene woman with misery belonging to me, I spread the tentacles of my wayward marriage.

"Millie," I said reluctantly, "my wife left this house six months ago. Without word to anyone I didn't care, but she came back last night. I've filed for divorce, but Shirley is hard to handle. Will you stay Millie? Bear with me, please, I'll do what I can to spare either one of us embarrassment and do promise, Shirley will not be living in this house."

"I heard muffled words last night, Ryan," Millie said. "I really didn't listen, but I do know that someone is using the spare bedroom. I'm glad you want me to stay, Ryan, I'm happy here. I enjoy looking after your son and I'll stay out of your way. The kitchen on my side will work for me. I'll stay in my apartment with Edward, just let me know which side you want to have meals.

"Thank you Millie, but Shirley will be difficult, don't let her upset you."

"I understand, Ryan. Not knowing your wife, my one wish is happiness for everybody, but will she let me care for Edward?"

"Millie, I'll hash that with Shirley today. If I have to carry her she will leave this house."

Meanwhile, Edward claimed attention. Millie fed the little guy, and pressed for time, I called the office.

"Dad," I said, "Shirley came home last night. I have a lot to say and I want answers."

"Take all the time you need son," dad said. "Mack has a slow day and I need time for phone calls. Straighten your life, Ryan, and call your mother, she would like to take Millie to lunch."

I've asked mom to take Millie shopping, dad. She's probably on her way," and just then Millie came in the kitchen with Edward.

"Well, we're ready," she said smiling? "The day should be nice, Edward likes outings, and I enjoy your mother's company."

"Mom likes being with you too, Millie and hardly having the words out of my mouth, Shirley barged into the kitchen.

"Well, what happened to my bathroom?" She demanded acidly. "I had one when I left."

Taking Edward with her, Millie, retreated to er apartment.

"Curb the crap, Shirley. You left more than a bath room when you walked out. I don't want you here."

"I've got news for you, Ryan, I'm not going anywhere," she rebelled, "this is my house as well as yours."

"You don't have anything to do with this building. You were out of this house just one week when I packed your belongings. You and your suitcases are going for a ride. You're in line for a summons, and that, you can't refuse."

Hearing mom's car in the drive, Millie heard too, and passing through the kitchen, she acknowledged a courteous "good morning."

Shirley didn't budge. Completely unmoved, she faced the wall never once looking at her son. I was shocked. That bit of apathy called for payback, and I couldn't wait. Mom did not come inside, Millie met her at the car, and fastening Edward in the safety seat, they drove away.

Consequently, Shirley had slept with her clothes on and taking advantage, I hurried my intentions.

"You're all dressed. That's fine. Now, get in the car!"

Grabbing the suitcases that I had packed six months before, I demanded, "Get in the car!"

Three times she defied me, but I was determined.

"Get in the car, Shirley, or suffer the consequence."

"No! I will not!" She yelled, "and damn the consequence!"

A scene at my front door, I didn't need, but knowing Shirley, she would create one. Striking my face, wildly, her fingernails dug into my lip, and tasting blood, I lost control. Slapping her face three times, satanically, she glared. The tantrum left her breathless, and realizing I was not going to take any more crap, she cooled. Forcing her to the car, I drove to her mother's house, hurled her suitcase on the porch, and forcing her from the car, I dragged the bitch across the lawn leaving her to cower in the grass. I didn't care if she had a key or if any one was there to let her in. I don't think I would have ever treated anyone so terrible, but with a stockpile of anger, Shirley managed to upset vehemence that had been swelling in my gut for months.

The following morning I smelled freshly brewed coffee that I couldn't wait to get to. Having no sleep the night before, I had trouble last night too, and concerned with the pile of work that waited for me at the office, I was aggravated with a lump in my chest.

Disregarding my aches, I managed altering six blueprints that should have been approved weeks before, and having no lunch, my stomach pinched. Millie had supper waiting when I came home. I served my plate and conscious of Shirley's repugnant behavior, Millie deserved an explanation.

Low in spirit, I smiled humbly. "I hope you had a good night's rest, Millie, I hardly closed my eyes."

"I'm sorry, Ryan," she mentioned sympathetically, then, wisely, overlooking what had happened, Millie adjusted to what might be a solution.

"Maybe you'd like to try something different. Take two Tylenol tablets, have a glass of warm milk and skip the nightly Regal."

Millie winked facetiously, but chiding had the ring of a true scold. Knowing I was humiliated, coyly, Millie added her two cents, and pithily explained, "that's a remedy for disturbed minds."

Planting diversion, I got the message. Judging wisely, Millie lightened my mind. I am not an alcoholic, Millie knows that, drinking a nightly beer, I used the excuse to "unwind, but tonight, I will take her advice.

"Ryan," she said rather hesitant, "Andrea called last night. Next Friday, being her birthday, she would like to visit, but I don't think this is a good time."

"Any time is good, Millie, I know what you're thinking, but please, don't let the incident with Shirley upset your plans. I'll make sure she doesn't interfere."

"I've been in my apartment all day. My door is not locked to your wife, but she has not been to see her son. I don't mean to pry, but I'm sure there's a reason.

"Millie, we'll have a discussion soon, right now, Shirley is a problem I have to deal with."

Neither of her parents had ever called, but Shirley was back and they should know.

Dumping her belongings on the porch, my mind wondered to the beginning of misery. Not ready to undertake responsibility that Shirley had forced upon me, I have never believed I am Edwards's father, and today, I want so much to know that I am.

Calculating the lucrative harvest from my apartments, and with marriage far from my mind, at twenty-three, I had planned my future. Things fell apart, and making matters worse, out of the blue, I'm told that Shirley is neurotic. It is possible, an affluent judge might grant Shirley custody, and is she capable? Will she care for a child as a mother should? I consider this and many other maybes concerning the child that I had denied, but Edward is my little boy. Involved for six months in a tempestuous marriage, I gave nothing and expected nothing, but Shirley grew restless, and to liberate a craving desire, lust, could very well be the affronting cause that tempted Shirley to abandon her son. My head whirled, but more was yet to come. Work on two office buildings came to a halt when dad was notified that titles were in dispute.

CHAPTER FOURTEEN

Edward reached his first birthday in 1967. Millie made a cake, my parents came to celebrate and fascinated with the single glow, that topped the cake, Edward frolicked happily seeming to understand the day was focused on him.

Working until 8:00 the next evening, I told Millie not to bother with supper. I ate at Jim's Chicken House on Carrollton Avenue, and turning to my old habit, the Falstaff I drank gave me a headache.

Getting home rather late, lights were on in the kitchen, and parking I wondered why. Did Shirley worm her way back? Millie may have let her inside, but with no callous scene in sight, I was pleasantly surprised.

"We've been waiting for you Ryan," Millie said as I opened the door. "I hope you don't mind, Andrea's been here since 3:00 o'clock. We've had dinner with your parents and just minutes ago we had tea and birthday cake.

Turning to her daughter, she said. "Andrea, this nice gentleman is Ryan Daniels."

Andrea flashed a lovely smile. Green eyes and chestnut tresses curled naturally about her face and admiring the sheik beige suite that outlined her figure, Millie's daughter was more than what I pictured.

"Nice meeting you, Andrea. I'm sorry I'm so dusty," I said, apologetically. "It's been a long day."

"Oh, please, don't apologize," she said, "I'm the one crashing your door."

Rummaging through her suitcase, retrieving a bottle, Andrea smiled in a special way.

"It's a small gift," she said, "for you."

"How thought full, Miss Monohan. I appreciate the gesture. If you are not too tired from your trip, I'll get decent and we can pop the cork."

That sounds nice," she said, "please call me Andrea, and if it's all right, may I say Ryan."

"That's fine," I winked cockily. "Give me twenty minutes."

Locking eyes with hers, my self assured housekeeper flashed a grin that would sway a Cherub and interpreting the scene, Millie was not fooled. Rushing my shower, I jumped into clean clothes and hurried to the kitchen.

"Mother asked me to tell you "good night" Ryan," Andrea said filling two pony shots with Amaretto. "I hope you won't mind having just me for company."

"I don't mind at all," I grinned glibly, "Millie seems to do everything right."

Of course, she does. That's what Millie had intended all along. I was pleased as punch, Andrea appealed to me from the beginning, and I did my best to impress her.

"Mother wrote about you, she told things that stirred my curiosity, I'd like to know you better. Can we talk for a while?"

Smiling, a small dimple in her cheek deepened, she seemed to glow, and feeling a rage of goose bumps, something, was beginning to happen. Giving Millie credit for a perfect rendezvous, we talked until 2:00 in the morning. Sweet liquor gave way to coffee. I brewed a fresh pot, and with leftover cake Andrea cut two pieces. Somehow, I was drawn, my heart beat with an unusual thump, and virile reflections were more than a thought.

The following morning I was in the kitchen before my alarm rang. Millie had the usual pot of coffee on the stove, pancakes and sausage were in the oven, she buttered three slices of toast and filling Edward's bottle with orange juice, she cockily smiled.

"You two must have had a long talk last night. Andrea is still asleep."

"We had a nice conversation, Millie, I've been expecting Andrea's visit, but you waited quite some time before inviting her."

"I know, Ryan. I thought it best not having Andrea sooner," she shrugged, "things were uncertain for a while."

"Andrea is a lovely girl, Millie," I said, "we had a pleasant evening."

"I'm glad, Ryan," she grinned. "I'm proud of Andrea, and thank you for the nice complement."

Stashing my dish in the sink, I grabbed a peek at Edward, and with a pile of work up front, I hurried to the office.

Blueprints for the drugstore were yet to be improved, but that shouldn't take long and waiting until noon, I phoned Andrea asking if she would have dinner with me.

"Thank you, Ryan" she said, "I'd like that," and assuming that she might enjoy the Court of Two Sisters restaurant in the quarter, I reserved a table. For the first time since Carol, my feelings veered to a woman and feeling like a man, Andrea was that woman.

CHAPTER FIFTEEN

The courtyard was convenient. Guided to a table near the fountain, Andrea liked the atmosphere, and offering a wine list the waiter suggested a cocktail.

"Would you like a Martini Andrea?" I asked.

"That sounds good," she said, "make mine dry."

Ordering two drinks alike, Andrea lifted the flute. "Here's to Ryan Daniels, this lovely restaurant and a wonderful city."

But something was left unsaid. I inspiration in her eyes seemed to tell me, and longing for love, it's now or never. Carol and Shirley were counter parts, looking in that direction, I grappled, but now, it's different. Andrea is important, I have good feelings for her, I want her to love me and be my wife, but .... there's Shirley.

"What are you thinking of Ryan?" Andrea asked. "You seem smothered in thought."

"I'm sorry Andrea, I didn't think it showed," and not realizing audacity, I muttered, "I'm thinking of how much I would like to love you. Does that shock you?"

"No, not really," she said. "I'm flattered, Ryan."

"Just two questions," I asked, "Are you in love with anyone, and is it possible that I might fit into your life?"

"Do you want spur-of-the-moment truth?" She asked.

"Just be honest." I shrugged.

Andrea shifted her eyes to mine. "I'm not engaged to anyone," she said, "call it infatuation, if you will, but I don't think so. From the core of my being, I want you to love me."

My smile broadened, "Andrea, I can't say it any other way. I've been on cloud nine since you've been here. I've never wanted anything more than to love you," and realizing, what she had so intrepidly inferred, I needed assurance.

"Would you consider going with me to a hotel?"

"More than anything, Ryan," she said.

"Mother has told me about your wife, she mentioned divorce, but should you decide otherwise, I'll accept whatever comes. Just believe, I love you."

"Andrea, I've never been so sure of any one, but divorce takes time. I've never loved Shirley. Let's not talk about that now, someday, I'll tell you the whole story."

"Your little boy is sweet, he is friendly, and mother loves him. I have patience Ryan, I'll wait."

In suite 165 at the hotel, kissing this wonderful woman, warmth from her body chilled my naked spine. Probing the crease of birth, Andrea endured pain, and seething with love that was meant to be, culmination was the grandest moment in my entire life.

"I've hurt you, I know. I'm sorry Andrea, I couldn't help my self."

"Shhh, I wanted it that way. Her hand touched my lips halting words that I wanted her to hear. Giving herself wholeheartedly, she endured pain and I, will never forsake virtuous glory.

Clinging, tenderly, she whispered.

"This night belongs to us. It's our Honeymoon."

Switching hours from 9:00 to 3:00 in the afternoon, I had more time for Andrea. Loving passionately, I enjoyed the taste of intimacy. I was never more lighthearted, but two weeks was not long enough.

Scheduled for 2:00 p.m. Andrea will leave tomorrow, I'm not happy about that and Millie is misty-eyed. Driving to the airport, I spotted Shirley's Chevrolet. Raymond Brock, my attorney, had served the divorce papers, and not looking forward to court procedure, I was uneasy. But why is Shirley spying on me? I'm sure Millie saw her too, but I don't think that Millie is concerned, she knows I'm in love with her daughter. Good-byes hurt, Millie cried a bit, and when the plane was out of sight, my mind drifted. Leaving my Alma Mata, it took a while to learn about love, Carol was realistic, but Shirley maneuvered a relationship exposing the role of an aggressive nymph.

CHAPTER SIXTEEN

Hazel is pregnant. Ben is on cloud nine, and eager to father a son, I wish him well. Me, huh! I'm footloose.

Waiting for my divorce to become final, I'm happier now than I have ever been, no one can burst that bubble and Saturday morning, just a few weeks after Andrea went back to Texas, a phone call from mom hit like a ton of bricks.

"Ryan," she mumbled uneasily. "Have you read the morning paper yet? It's on page twenty, the obituary column."

"No, I haven't mom. What's going on?"

"Ryan, Mr. Freeman died two days ago. I'm sure there's just one Franklin Pierce Freeman, husband of Mona Freeman, father to Shirley and Michael. It's so shocking, I can hardly believe what I've read."

"It's true mom," I said reading the details. "We are estranged families, but I don't see how this can be ignored. Do you think I should call?"

"Let me handle it, Ryan. I think women have a better approach to sympathy."

"Do what you think best, mom, I would be uncomfortable at the funeral. I can't handle things like that."

Mom and dad attending the funeral, long before now, I had lost respect and feeling deceived, simply, I sent flowers.

Two weeks, battling with steady repairs, I mopped, seeming to just drag around, and paying her usual Saturday morning visit, mom noticed my listless stride.

"Ryan," she suggested, "it's early. "why don't we take Edward on a picnic?"

Edward liked outings especially, City Park, and to wade in the pool, mom shopped at the mall for red Superman trunks. Millie made potato salad and sandwiches. Mom fried a few chicken thighs and packing the ice-chest with soft drinks and water, I shoved plastic utensils, paper plates and cups in the basket. Waiting for Millie to dress Edward. the doorbell rang.

"Let me in, Ryan, we have to talk." Shirley said standing dogmatically in the doorway.

"Cripes, Shirley, you're filled with surprises. What's the beef now?"

"Ryan, in all fairness, you should know why I left," she said shoving past me. "The way things were I could not give my son the love he deserved."

"Really? You smothered me!" I spate harshly.

Carelessly throwing her purse on a chair, the corner of her mouth twisted, surely, she would cause trouble, and not prepared for an outburst, I softened.

"I'm sorry about your father, Shirley. You have my sympathy."

"I don't want your sympathy, and vehemently, squinting her eyes, she shrieked "I'm glad he's dead! He's the beast that raped me! The child in this house belongs to my father!"

"Really?" I said without caring. No matter how, Shirley had a way getting attention.

"That's a terrible accusation, Shirley. Unfortunately, the man isn't here to defend himself. Is revenge that sweet? I don't believe you."

"Why couldn't you love me, Ryan?" she implored "I've been miserable loving you."

In the blink of an eye, her arms locked around me, kissing hard, her teeth cut into my lip, then, probing wildly in her purse, she pulled a gun.

"Live with it, Ryan, if you can," then, pointing the nozzle to her throat, she pulled the trigger.

Crumbled on the kitchen floor, a halo of blood encircled her head, the appalling sight left me rigid, my blood chilled, I could not move, and coming to my senses, Millie was sponging my face, with an icy cloth.

"Ryan" she said, with a shot of whiskey in her hand, "You'd best drink this, and call the police."

Arrested as a suspect, I spent forty-eight hours in lock-up, and not finding my fingerprints on the gun, I was released.

Early the next morning, I called Andrea, relating all that had happened.

"Will you come, Andrea? I'm asking you to marry me."

"Give me a week, darling," she said excited. "I'll give the usual notice and book the first plane I can get."

Waiting for Andrea, I did not use the kitchen, and wanting her to have a new home, I scanned a fairly new subdivision in the Lake View area. Mom liked the eight room house that I had selected, Millie did too, and just down the street, a shopping mall was taking shape. With help from my parents, moveable objects were packed, furniture and drapes, were left to Andrea, and eight days after my call we were married. Andrea was interested in her home, she insisting we postpone our Honeymoon, and furnish the house. Choosing mahogany, oak and maple for bedrooms, Andrea selected a plush sofa set for the den, tailored drapes covered twenty windows and having laid beige carpet, my wife worked well around color.

Within two years, Edward had a little brother, Glen Elliot Daniels is three and there are times when big brother broadens authority.

"Edward, your little brother needs your help. He doesn't know all the things that you know. You should teach him. Tell him what is right and what is wrong and you two will always be friends."

Understanding what responsibility means, Edward, you deserve authority, but not too demanding.

A year later the subdivision bubbled. The mall was fashionable, stores were reputable, and holding to tradition, "Goldrings" and "Maison Blanche" were exclusive. Gazing at the breezy garment displayed on a mannequin, surely, Andrea would like the pink nightgown. Tucking the package under my arm, I hurried to my car, Mrs. Freeman was parking next to where I was and deep down. I did not want her to see me.

"Hello, Ryan, how is my grandson?" She scoffed.

Provoked with her attitude, I almost bit my tongue, instead, I answered respectfully.

"It's nice seeing you, Mrs. Freeman." I said. "You can visit any time you wish. Edward will be eight years old in two weeks."

Dropping her head, I noticed regret. Quickly, she apologized, and doing so, she humbly, explained.

"I'm sorry Ryan, I've been living with remorse for some time. I'd like very much to see Edward. Do you really mean what you've just said?"

"Of course, I do, Mrs. Freeman. I know you've been hurt, we all have, but why stick to a grudge? Families should be sociable."

"Ryan, I've been wanting to tell you, the autopsy was evidence. Shirley had a malignant brain tumor. I think that's why she committed suicide. We didn't realize that and neither did the doctor."

"My God!" I said shocked, and with the swiftness of a whiplash, I realized how much this ill-fated girl suffered. Sympathizing, not just for her mother, Shirley did not deserve the torment, and I, am guilty as well.

CHAPTER SEVENTEEN

June 20, 1975, Andrea planned a party inviting ten neighboring children, and considering the Mexican standoff, she mentioned "a birthday party might lighten the chill."

"Ryan," she said, "surely, Edward has to know his grandmother, but before I go too far, I want your permission. "Is it all right to invite Mrs. Freeman to the party?"

"Of course, Andrea. The invitation might bring us together. Call her, she has reason to come."

Children arrived early, Mrs. Freeman came minutes later, and especially attached to the walking robot that she brought, Edward was elated. Not having seen her grandson for many years, Mrs. Freeman cavorted happily pinning the tail on the donkey. Andrea snapped a roll of film, and when the party was over, a social get-together at dinner seemed to heal yesterday's wounds. Millie surprised the coffee hour with cup cakes and sipping Crème de Menthe, credible conversation seemed to harmonize anguish from the past.

Setting the scene, we uncovered what had to be. Edward fell asleep on the divan, Mrs. Freeman kissed his cheek, and before leaving, noticed a tear. I carried him to his bed and content with what the evening seemed to enforce, grandmother Freeman was no longer a stranger. Millie retired to her room, and soothing a family rift, Andrea relaxed in my arms.

"Ryan, much time has passed, and still, I love you."

She said playfully.

Kissing her chin, I said. "I'm easy to love, my pet. Stay the way you are, I remarked, "but don't take too much for granted."

"Ryan, seriously, I'm thinking of Edward, the child deserves honesty. Shouldn't we talk to him? Adoption is complicated, especially for a little boy, and another point, my love, I don't think we should tell. Isn't it better to ask?"

"If you wish," I said, "Edward is bright, he'll understand."

The very next day, confronting Edward, I spoke hesitantly. "Edward, "Mommy and I have been wanting to talk with you for some time, but you were too young to understand. You're eight now, but listen carefully."

"Sure, dad. Are you going to tell me a story?" He asked.

"In a way, son, it is a story. A story about you and your real mother."

"You told me my real mother was with God," he reminded.

"Yes, Edward, your real mother is with God. Learning about God in Sunday school gives you a good start, but you must be honest with yourself."

Squinting, a bit, he looked perplexed, surely, he had questions and keeping matters simple, I explained.

"Edward, do you remember when you were five years old, the time Andrea and I were married? I asked if you would like to call like to call Andrea Mommy?

"Sure, I do, Dad. You told me that "Mommy" was your pet name for Andrea."

"Do you love Mommy Edward?" I asked.

"Sure, dad, Mommy makes good cookies."

"Try to understand, son. Mommy has been looking after you ever since you were three years old, and now, she would like to adopt you."

"Gee, dad, what does that mean?" He asked.

Seeing me at a disadvantage, Andrea took the bull by the horns.

"Edward, I love you very much," she said looking into his eyes. "Just as I ask to adopt you, I'm asking you to adopt me. If you like the idea, it simply means that you will be my legal son, and I will be your legal mother. When this is done, law books will show, when I go with God, all that belongs to me will legally belong to you and dad."

"Gee, Mommy," he said smiling, "does that mean I can have your car?"

"Of course, darling, but you won't want mine. When you learn to drive dad will buy a new one for you. Are you willing to have me as your legal mother?"

"Sure, Mommy," he said smiling. "I always thought you were my mother."

Sentiment touched my heart. I choked. Andrea shed a quiet tear, and embracing our son, emotion ripped me to little pieces. Keeping things simple, Edward seemed pleased, and becoming a man, life, will bolster the rest.

CHAPTER EIGHTEEN

Until today, the horror of Shirley's suicide and what she said sticks in my gut like a burr. Andrea knows just what I told her years ago, but she should know the truth. During the night, she cuddled, embracing my body, she looked for love, but with a boggled mind, now was not a good time.

"Andrea, darling, can we talk?" I quickly asked.

"Of course, darling. Are you in another of your moods? I know I'm prying, but please, tell me. Why do you brood so much? What is it that bothers you? Is it something financial, something you don't want me to know?"

"No, my love. nothing like that. What I want to talk about is far from a matter of money. It's more like a plague."

"Talking might help, my darling. It's getting so, we don't have much to talk about."

"Andrea, I'm going to pour my guts. Please, try to understand. If you can help, talk to me openly."

I could not look into her face and lowering my head, humility merged with confession.

"Andrea, though I love the child, I cannot bring myself to believe Edward is my son. Just before Shirley pulled the trigger, she said it was her father who raped her and with that, well, that's another thing. I've been thinking, maybe I should confront her mother, but I don't know where to begin. What do you think I should do?"

Andrea did not flinch, looking directly at me, she seemed to be putting two with two, and with limited hesitance, she triggered an answer.

"Ryan, have that talk. Let Mrs. Freeman know the despicable means that put an end to her daughter's life. Get it off your chest. It's the only way."

The next evening Mrs. Freeman offered me inside her home, but tackling head on, I was leery. Bitter conversation would make matters worse, and if she does know, will she tell me?

"Mrs. Freeman, I've been living with this for years not knowing how to handle it, but it's time you knew. Shirley came to me pregnant, accusing me of being the father of her unborn child, but before committing suicide, she said her father was the one who raped her. Her exact words were, *"Ryan, it's not your fault, but sex with you, solved the problem. You must believe me, My father is Edward's father too."* With much regret, Mrs. Freeman, what I have just said is true."

Brushing a tear, the lady winced, her face twisted painfully, and why should Shirley dare to expose a lie so sadistic.

"Ryan," Mrs. Freeman explained, "I'm truly lost hearing something so terrible, especially from the child that I have reared and loved, but I'm not sorry that you have confronted me. Shirley was rebellious, a difficult child to raise. We have never discussed sticky situations, Shirley told little white lies more often than necessary, and thinking like parents, we blamed childish fantasy. I should be angry, but I'm not. Above all, you should be the one to know."

"Ryan," she said soberly, "Shirley and David were adopted, my husband was sterile. The one reason I can contributed to the far out discrepancies that Shirley dreamed is to blame the tumor we didn't know she had. Try to forgive her Ryan. Deep in my heart, I know she loved you. Hurting, so much when you turned your back, it could be she needed something to take with her. Lying to you was a ticket to revenge, and with that, she took her life. This isn't easy for me either, but it's over. You have the truth now Ryan. Should you want more satisfaction, you can talk to Doctor Scott, he has all the records."

Surprised and shocked, I didn't expect what Mrs. Freeman had so ordinarily explained, but picturing the safety pin that had so noticeably fallen from Shirley's purse, *Surely, Edward is of my genes. I do have a son.*

CHAPTER NINETEEN

"Dad," Edward said barging into the den. "I've finished the puzzle that Mommy bought. Will you help me paste it together? I have four pictures in my room now and there's room for two more."

Never before have I been so proud. Always, Edward has called me "dad," but today, the title rang true.

Celebrating another anniversary, Andrea and I have been together for ten years, three children are our pride and joy, and family oriented, we enjoy life. Assets have improved, dad is looking forward to retirement, mom is in the best of health, and living with a clear conscience, I have never been so relaxed. Mrs. Freeman is one of the family. Shirley's malice kept us apart for too long. Cultivating friendship, the lone lady is a gem, and we wouldn't have it any other way.

THE END